CONTENTS

ACKNOWLEDGMENTS

This book took me much longer to write than it feels like it should have. Many, many people have helped me since I started writing it, not with the book necessarily but with living my life which is probably even more important. I would like to start with a big thanks to them. I would also like to thank all the amazing economists, historians, psychologists, anthropologists, political scientists, other scientists, researchers, sci-fi writers and movie directors whose work and ideas have informed and inspired this book and who are mostly listed in the back. Specifically, I would like to thank the following people who have helped me polish it into something you will hopefully enjoy reading. For this I would like to thank Patrick, Corinna, Antonio, Leandro, Estela, Sally and Freddy. Finally, for being there throughout, for supporting, inspiring and challenging me and for generally just making life really nice, I would like to thank Tine and Casper.

I hope you enjoy the book.

CHAPTER ONE

INTRODUCTION

Science fiction is a way of imagining how things might change as a result of some scientific discovery or development. Science fiction writers try and represent how this change might impact the world by combining what they know with calculated guesses, conjecture, and a little bit of fantasy. Gene Rodenberry imagined how the galactic federation of planets might interact with an intelligent species inhabiting a newly discovered world.[1] One of the earliest recognised works of science fiction, Mary Shelley's Frankenstein, imagined what might happen if a scientist developed the technology to bring the dead back to life.[2]

Economists are a bit like science fiction writers. There is a lot we know about how the economy works. But there is also a lot we don't know. On the surface, the economy seems to make sense. People go to work, they run businesses, they buy and sell stuff – it's simple. But when you look beyond this seemingly stable surface view, the human economy might just be the most complex thing in the (known) universe. Chess has sixteen pieces moving one at a time, in a rule-based fashion, across an eight-by-eight board and a game of chess can play out in more ways than there are atoms in the universe. Yet this is nothing compared to how millions or billions of self-directed human beings, their objects and their institutions act and interact – with free will – across a relatively unbounded space within a human economy. Economists must therefore combine what they know with calculated guesses, conjecture, and a little bit of fantasy to understand what's happening in the economy, and how it might be impacted by a particular change or policy.

If we made a sci-fi movie with the central premise that we fully understood the economy, it would quickly turn dark. A fascist dictator or evil corporation would take control of the invisible hand and direct its power to their own ends. That's always a risk with any new scientific development – particularly in the movies. But if we could fully understand our economy, in a way that served our values as a society, we could achieve some truly amazing things.

Our most valuable possession

An economy is our birthright. It is the web of physical,

social and intellectual structures that our mothers and fathers, grandparents, great grandparents and beyond, imagined, refined and maintained. It fed, clothed and sustained them, and it continues to sustain us today as we exchange the product of our own efforts for the things we need to survive and flourish. If we're lucky, our ancestors might bequeath us money, land or maybe a baseball card collection. We might be born an Ecclestone or the next Sultan of Brunei and generally not have terribly much to worry about. But if there is one thing that most of us can thank or blame our ancestors for, it is the economic world that they have left behind.

Individually our forebears might have helped to build a bridge, improve a design or refine a process. Or they might have fed, clothed or provided shelter to others who did. Perhaps they fought for economic freedom, walked the streets in protest against an overbearing government, demanded lower taxes, higher wages, a shorter working week or better working conditions. Some will have contributed more than others, some may have taken more than they put in, but together, past and present generations have provided for every man-made thing around us. There are those things we can still touch; the buildings, the roads, the infrastructure. There are contributions we can only see the results of; the countless hours of thought and effort that have furthered our understanding and capabilities and from which everything not of this natural world emerges.

This is an effort which dates back beyond generations. It is not an accumulation of fortunate coincidences, it is a force of nature set in motion a long time ago, like the expansion of the universe or the orbit of the moon. At some point in the past, we accumulated a small number of biological and social advantages that gave us the ability to interact with and control our environment like no species that went before us. Driven by our fears and desires and facilitated by human capabilities, we have been advancing this mastery ever since. Its advance can be destructive for many in the short term. Individuals who benefit from the way things have traditionally been done, driven by the same fears and desires, will often try to stop it, or direct it where they want it to go. Throughout history they have delayed its effects, sometimes intentionally for their own benefit, sometimes in the belief that their actions form part of the continuing advance.

Where and when we are born determines whether we live in a time of progress, stagnation or regression. Much like being born into a bitter ice age, crippling drought or a temperate climate and abundant resources, the social/political/economic climate we are born into can make our lives easier or a whole lot harder.

Life is struggle – at the cellular level, in the schoolyard, in the workplace. We each have our own problems to solve, and they are complicated and consuming enough that we don't often have the time to think too much about the contribution we might be making to the march of progress, or how our actions might further mould and shape the economy we are a small part of. We tend to be so busy doing what we can to survive and then hopefully enjoying ourselves a little, that there's not a lot of time to figure out how to make the world a better place.

Thankfully for both progress and humanity, it is predominantly in the act of surviving, the act of feeding and protecting ourselves and our families, of staying alive, seeking satisfaction and pursuing our desires over time that, little by little, progress... progresses. As human beings we have the capacity, more than any other creature, to adapt our behaviour to our environment, to look for better ways of doing things and then, through the benefit of some of our earlier achievements, to pass those improvements onto others who can refine them further. We generally don't need to manage or facilitate this process, it is what we do, it's what we've always done.

We do have a long way to go. We get hungry, we fear, we fall, we get sick, we die. After millions of years of trying, there are still many problems to overcome. We continue, therefore, to search for small solutions and we continue to progress. But sometimes we are impatient, looking to where we want to be and wondering why we are not there already. Blame is laid at various places, often at the feet of those very processes that got us to where we are today. We look to control the economy, to extract more out of it or perhaps to lessen its destructive aspect. But there are a number of things that make this very, very challenging.

It's really complex

The fundamental components of any economy are human beings – and we are notoriously complex and unpredictable in isolation. An economy involves human beings interacting and transacting, not just with family or close friends, but with other people and often with complete strangers, including people of different ages, values and cultures. We do this via an incredibly complex network of technologies, traditions and institutions, each of which have their own peculiarities. These artefacts of human society form the network infrastructure upon which economic activity takes place.

Layered on top of an already complex economy is a financial system which often (and frequently intentionally) distorts our perception of the real economy, much like a pool of water chopped up by the wind. An economy is living, breathing humans occupying a massive, complex, part man-made, part natural world; a dynamic, pulsing, unpredictable system, within which the outcome of seemingly simple changes can be very difficult to predict, with occasional extraordinary and unexpected consequences.

Change is scary

Economics is about the battle for scarce resources, and everyone is at war. Workers, shareholders, taxpayers, public servants, retirees, university students, school children, people that haven't even been born yet. We are, rightfully, very protective of our economy and wary of changes that we fear might reduce our access to resources. Economic policies ideally provide an overall net benefit, but they are not without cost. Things like improved services or infrastructure cost money and some people will perceive them as not being worth the expense. Reducing services or infrastructure might mean the loss of a benefit that others have come to value. Sometimes policies that ultimately increase overall output or resources result in a redistribution from one group to another. Where one group loses out, or doesn't gain as much as another, they might object to the change. But we have come as far as we have, mostly as a consequence of small steps which collectively bring us forward over time, even as some are of little or even negative benefit to certain groups or individuals.

It's constantly changing

An economy is dynamic. It is made up of individual components that think and react to the decisions and actions of other components. If an individual has an idea that could improve aspects of the economy and can get it past those who are likely to oppose the change, then there's no guarantee that it's going to be effective for long. Every other individual component of the economy on their own quest for survival will adapt, compete and innovate to try to make the change work for their benefit, often remoulding and reshaping the world into something that no longer resembles the one for which the change was originally conceived.

What's right?

Because economic decisions can have negative consequences for some groups, we often have to make difficult choices. The benefit a government can pay out or the services it can provide have to be weighed against how much it can take from its citizens in taxes, for example. There are intangible components of economic policy; social harmony, clean air and biodiversity, which don't belong to anyone despite being immensely valuable. An undefined, unallocated and unprotected resource will generally be taken advantage of. But it's also hard to convince someone freezing to death to not chop down a tree to start a fire. Choosing what is right is hard and the decision-making processes are messy and imperfect. The argument that prevails is not necessarily based on careful analysis of the policies or actions that will lead to an optimal outcome. Economic decisions are based on a mix of science, logic and objective analysis, combined with emotions, sales, marketing and politics.

Short or long term

In line with the above, most economic decisions involve some trade-off between the short term and the long term. Choosing for one, means choosing against the other. Money borrowed by governments today increases the burden on future taxpayers. Money saved by governments today through increased taxation might reduce the burden on future taxpayers at the cost of those paying taxes today. An industry subsidised today may protect jobs temporarily while eroding competitiveness and efficiency over the long term. We tend to be very much about the present. If we get something now it's ours, we can do what we want with it. If someone offers to give us something in the future, we must first delay gratification or endure the doubt that we will actually get what we have been promised.

And yet, while we might have a general preference for more immediate gratification, if fear of the future consequences of our actions is strong enough, we can often be convinced to wait. In its reactionary complexity, however, choosing not to take a course of action in the present for fear of messing up the future could be precisely what leads to the future being messed up.

Why try?

We see an economy in motion at a point in its evolution and may think it can be left well enough alone. But the economy, like the institutions it is partially comprised of, is a work under perpetual construction and renovation. It was set in motion long ago, tossed and turned throughout history, fretted, fussed and fought over today. It is what it is, for better and worse, because of our intrusions.

Philosopher and economist John Stuart Mill said, "Bad men need nothing more to compass their ends, than that good men should look on and do nothing."[3] People are always trying to change or control the economy. This can include imposing restrictions on others, taking things that don't belong to them or gaining an advantage at someone else's expense. The level of economic freedom, of historically relative equal access to opportunity that many of us enjoy today had to be fought for. Economic freedom results from our own accumulated efforts to maintain an economy that is a resource we can all engage with. The economy is too valuable to be left alone – and not because it needs us to tell it what to do. If we're not actively and continuously trying to understand and preserve it as a resource that works to provide for us all, you can guarantee someone else will make it work for them instead.

Horrified by its ugliness, Frankenstein shunned his creation. As a result, the creature felt abandoned and betrayed and set about killing the people Frankenstein cared for most.

An economy is not going to seek revenge on us if we don't care for it. But it is our collective creation, it is incredibly powerful and of immense benefit to us all. After Frankenstein tracks down his monster, he confronts and intends to kill it. The creature implores of him, "Do your duty towards me, and I will do mine towards you and the rest of mankind."[2]

CHAPTER TWO

THE FIGHT

There's approximately 100 billion stars and perhaps 400 billion planets in the Milky Way galaxy. There are approximately one trillion galaxies in the universe. In 1950 Enrico Fermi asked his colleagues, "where is everybody?"[1] It wasn't a joke – he really wanted to know. With that many stars and planets out there, and with life literally all around us, he didn't understand why we hadn't seen any evidence of life outside our planet. Not necessarily visiting aliens, but radio waves, remnants of the past, or evidence of the continuing existence of life somewhere in the universe. In 1961, to stimulate conversation, Frank Drake wrote a famous equation which estimated how many planets in the Milky Way could be home to a form of life, and technologically advanced enough to produce evidence of their existence.[2] The highest reasonably founded estimates suggest there could be up to 15 million planets. 15 million sounds like a lot, and it's probably too high, but it would mean approximately 1 in every 27,000 planets may contain intelligent life. Other estimates, equally as reasonable, suggest that the number of planets home to intelligent life in the Milky Way, aside from Earth, could actually be zero.

All living things that have existed over a period of time or which still continue to exist today have overcome ridiculously terrible odds to survive in a universe that was not designed for them but which, across its infinite size and complexity, has thrown a rare few comparatively miniscule environments within which life can appear, if everything is just right, from nowhere. Once they've managed to make it into existence in the first place, every living thing is food or a potential threat for another, or many, living things. The emergence and continuing existence of a species of complex living beings is a miracle beyond biblical proportions. So, while the species of this earth are vastly diverse in terms of appearance, behaviours and mechanisms that they rely on to ensure their own survival, there is one thing they all have in common. They are all born to fight, to fight for their own survival in most cases, but more importantly to fight for the existence of their own kind. It is the single unifying feature of all living things, even the ones that we don't know about. That something could have existed without this characteristic will probably never become apparent to us, because if it ever did emerge, it would not have survived for long.

Our own personal battle for survival is evidenced by a number of things that we cannot do without. We must breathe, drink, eat and sleep (if we don't sleep it becomes very hard to find something to eat). We must have the help and support of others, as without their dedicated attention we would be dead within hours of our birth. Luckily, we also generally want to support and help others, starting with those we are related to. We really, really want to have sex (another act necessary for our survival).

We are driven to do these things through a complex web of biological and emotional processes, most of which we are not even consciously aware of. They emerge as urges, wants, desires and fears. We avoid pain and the things we fear will cause it. We seek out pleasure and joy and things that make us feel good. These drivers have defined our behaviours since long before we were genetically human. We are privileged to be able to understand many of them, but that does not change the fears and desires themselves. Every decision that we make and everything that we do is driven by these factors.

Beyond the challenges of surviving another day we, as humans, have managed to reach a point in which our continuation as a species is secure – aside from a global catastrophe. Our immediate environment does not threaten us. Those born even just a hundred years ago had a 1 in 100 chance of living to 100, today it's about 1 in 3-4.[3] Our old, sick and frail are cared for, and the average 20 year old woman has a .04% chance of dying in the next year (it's higher for men but we still have cause for optimism).[4] Modern maladies are often problems of excess. Too much of the wrong foods, drinks or drugs, too much pollution, or existential issues associated with too much choice, time or conflict over which desire we wish to satisfy next. These issues, while certainly problems of their own kind, are ones which most other species, if they were capable of conceptualising such a transaction, would joyfully swap their own hardships for. They are certainly problems that the majority of our ancestors would be proud to have bequeathed to us.

There are a few key things that have enabled us to achieve this privileged position. We are blessed with a number of anatomical advantages. We have opposable thumbs. We have complex vocal cords that enable us to communicate through a diverse range of sounds. We have a cooling system that enables us to run for hours on end without having to stop to pant.[5] But our anatomy probably isn't the main key to our success. Compared to other animals of our size, we are slow and weak. I can't think of many animals anywhere near my size that I would feel comfortable facing up against in a fight (or a 100-metre sprint). I don't imagine that my teeth and limited bite size could lock in and tear the flesh from many living animals, and my claws bend and crack when they grow more than three or four millimetres beyond my fingertips. Our bodies have brought us a long way, but the things that truly separate us from the other creatures around us are our brains, our societies, and our accumulated technologies.

Brains

As a proportion of our overall size, our brains are large when compared against those of most other animals. They're about twice the size of that of a bottlenose dolphin and three times the size of a chimpanzee (and they're both pretty clever). Perhaps more importantly, our brains have more neurons in the cerebral cortex (the area responsible for things like thinking, memory and language) than any other animal.[6] Human brains are a very expensive luxury. Most vertebrate species devote between 2 to 8% of their overall energy consumption to powering their brains.[7] The human brain typically consumes 20 to 25% of our total energy supply, or as much as 60% in infants.[8] Such a big investment would need to see a significant return in order to be worthwhile – and seemingly it does. We have more than 6,000 thoughts per day and can remember up to 10,000 faces (including 90% of the people we went to school with, 35 years after we left).[9] [10] We can create hundreds of different facial expressions to express how we feel and we can read and understand the expressions of others, even those that we have never met before. We can (with a little practice) automatically calculate the direction, arc and velocity required to hit a target moving at considerable speed with a stone or spear. We also have clearly advanced capacities in terms of memory, planning, reasoning, abstract thinking and communication. We can imagine things or behaviours that don't exist and bring them into existence. We can incorporate the ideas and improvements of others into our own lives, and we can transport those improvements over time and space. This enables us (or at least some of us) to compose symphonies, create near perfect visual replicas of the things we see around us, and design buildings that stand for generations. We can do all this while unconsciously coordinating the many physiological processes necessary to keep us alive. In a recent experiment, the world's fourth fastest supercomputer took 40 minutes while running 82,944 processors to replicate 1 second's worth of human brain activity.[11] Overall, our brains more than compensate for our undersized teeth and long skinny limbs.

Societies

Our brains also enable us to negotiate incredibly complex social structures, from family and friendship groupings through to workplaces, clubs, and body corporate meetings – all placed within a larger mix of groups numbering in the thousands and ultimately millions of individuals. It's difficult to say which came first, our magnificent brains or our astounding social structures. Without the brain we would not be able to navigate such systems and yet it is very likely that many of the characteristics of the human brain have been selected because they enabled us to operate within and enjoy the benefits of larger social groups.

Life would be a pretty miserable thing to go through alone. There also tends to be some real practical advantages associated with operating in groups rather than as individuals. We have been functioning in groups and benefiting from strength in numbers since the birth of our distant genetic ancestors. The benefits for modern humans are also pretty obvious. We can warn and protect each other from danger. We can care for each other when we are sick or can't get enough to eat, or we can build skyscrapers hundreds of metres into the sky and build rockets that fly to the moon.

For most of human history – excluding the last several thousand years – we lived in relatively small nomadic hunter-gatherer groups consisting of as few as 25 and up to several hundred individuals.[12] This was the number that our lifestyles and communities (restrained by babies, who can't walk until 2 years of age or feed themselves until about 8) would permit. This group size appears to have been optimal for the needs of ancient humans. We could watch out for and mount a significant defence against most threats. We were able to gather enough food to feed the entire group including children, the sick and the old, without stretching our resources too thin. It also appears to have provided sufficient diversity to ensure that genetic weaknesses did not become too highly concentrated. According to anthropologist Alan Dunbar, 150 people is also the maximum number of individuals that we can maintain meaningful relationships with.[13] Cognitively we find it difficult to keep track of the interactions and interrelationships of larger groups. 150 might sound like a small number given the things we are otherwise capable of, but there are actually 11,325 interconnections in a group of 150 individuals (and many more when you count interrelation of families, cliques and subgroups).

We support and are supported by other people, but our own objectives are not totally subordinated to those of the group. We need other people, but we still want to maximise our own share of the group's resources (for ourselves and for the people closest to us). Being an integrated yet individually successful group member requires us to understand who is connected to who – and how, what subgroups there are, subgroup dynamics, who's holding a grudge or who's sleeping with who, etc. We need to understand who would have our backs in which situation and how we might be able to improve those odds. At this level of detail 150 suddenly sounds like a pretty impressive number of people to keep track of.

There are physical benefits to working together, but larger group sizes also contribute to what we can achieve cognitively. Two heads are literally better than one. Steven Johnson has popularised the belief that the increasing pace of technological advancement is founded in the ever-increasing complexity of our interconnectedness. When individuals come together, thoughts and ideas interact and multiply.[14]

The gradual shift to farming approximately 10-12

thousand years ago increased the number of individuals that could be sustained within a defined space and the size of our communities increased. Larger group size leads to increased strength and resources in the battle for survival, and it permitted and required more and more complex interactions and activities within the group. Small increases in output meant that individuals had to put less effort into feeding themselves and their families, allowing them to put more effort into other activities such as tool or weapon making, which would further support the continuing growth, safety and wellbeing of the group.

Growth

While farming may have permitted larger numbers of people to congregate together, it did not instantly transform our long ingrained psychological preference for a more modest group size. Despite the benefits there are also real disadvantages to larger groups. Many groups resisted fully converting to this new lifestyle. We know this from the pattern with which agriculture emerged and spread across the globe. We also know it from the continuing existence of many groups who did not – and some that still have not – taken to farming despite the fact that they undoubtedly came into contact with and could have adopted agricultural lifestyles and larger communities.

Even a small group requires a set of "rules" that group members must abide by for it to function effectively. The most ancient of these rules are deeply wired into our DNA and are universal across all races. The experience of emotions; love, joy, fear, and anger, the ability to understand the perceptions and emotions of others, the awareness of and adherence to principles such as fairness, reciprocity, altruism and retribution, are all core human traits. Our brains, for example, contain mirror neurons that fire as though we ourselves are suffering when we see another human suffer. This causes feelings of empathy and increases our desire to support and help others. These emotions and sensitivities were the hard-coded rules that determined how ancient humans interacted together.[15]

In the Ultimatum Game, two people are offered $100. One of the pair gets to decide how the money is to be split; if they want, they can take the full $100 for themselves. The catch is that the second person must approve of the split, or they both receive nothing.[16 17 18] Rational economic theory would suggest that the second person should accept even a very low share of the money (say $1) because that's still more than what they would get if they rejected it. But in diverse societies all over the world, from the San tribes people to New York cab drivers, men and women of all ages, people tend to offer a "fair" split of approximately $50 each and offers of less than $20 are usually rejected. Logic dictates that if a stranger offers you a dollar (suspicion aside) that you should accept it regardless of how much they might keep for themselves. You will likely never see this person again and damaging them out of pure spite while short-changing yourself a dollar makes no sense. However, the reality is that our brains are not wired for doing deals with strangers in contrived laboratory settings. Rather, they are wired for interactions within a complex social network. If you and your best mate, or cousin or neighbour were offered this same deal and they offered you a dollar it suddenly makes more sense to knock them back. That is because the people we are used to dealing with are not strangers we will never see again, but people we interact with on a regular basis. We may not be given a free $100 to split between us very often, but there will likely be many occasions where we will want these people to take our own needs and desires into account alongside their own. A dollar is suddenly a small price to pay to impart an important lesson to the people around us.

While the lives of ancient humans were not likely to have been violence free, they were probably not as violent as we may imagine. Although there would have been in-group tensions, rivalries and occasional fights, our psychological evolution has laid the foundation for living mostly harmoniously in groups of up to 150 individuals. All members of a group of this size, made up of smaller interconnected family units, would know each other intimately.* Almost all matters would pertain to family or close associates and it would be in everyone's best interest to maintain harmony. There would have been very little between-group mobility as there wasn't a whole lot of us around, and rejection from your own group would have been an almost unbearable punishment. There was no such thing as anonymity; if a "crime" was committed it would have been very difficult for the perpetrator to escape detection or to move on to somewhere else. Negative consequences from a person's action would also almost always be impacting someone that they knew and probably cared about, further increasing the motivation to do the right thing.[19] Prior to the development of agriculture, the entire concept of personal possessions was also very different. Previously an individual's belongings had consisted of whatever they could carry on their backs. While some items would still have been very valuable to the individual, they were less valuable and less difficult to replace than the types or quantities of items able to be accumulated in a less nomadic lifestyle.

* There may not have even been distinct family units. In some societies it was believed that a child was not born of a single father, and a pregnant woman would continue having sex with multiple partners throughout her pregnancy in order to gather the best traits of the available males into her unborn child.

We appear to be hard-wired to work together, but we are probably hard-wired to work together in groups of something around this size. Groups significantly larger than 150 tend to have reduced levels of social cohesion and social harmony. There is a direct correlation between the size of towns or cities and their crime levels, beyond what could be expected due to an increase in population. More people equals more strangers, more people to distrust, and perhaps more real – or at least perceived – danger from other humans. Individuals can get lost both literally and metaphorically within large groups and people often feel more isolated and disconnected in large cities than they do in small towns. There are likely to be other additional reasons. Humans were generally well provided for by the hunter-gatherer lifestyle. The San of southern Africa are considered a reasonable modern representation of what the ancient hunter-gatherer lifestyle entailed, with evidence to suggest that they had it pretty good. The San today enjoy a nutritionally diverse diet only recently surpassed by modern man and a level of leisure time still the envy of modern labour organisations (it is estimated that they spend between 12 to 19 hours per week on food gathering activities).[20] [21] According to Jared Diamond, when one tribe member was asked why his tribe had not taken up agriculture, he responded, "Why should we, when there are so many mongongo nuts in the world?"[22] Farming remains a volatile business to this day and early agriculture would have had many additional pitfalls. Early farmers probably went through a long and hazardous learning phase. Evidence suggests that many groups initially alternated between farming and hunting for many years before agriculture became dominant. The transition into farming probably saw the loss of much knowledge and many skills critical to the hunter-gatherer lifestyle. It also saw a congregation of individuals into areas incapable of supporting their number without farming. Farming by nature usually results in a concentration of effort into a smaller range of plants and animals. This can increase the risk to the food supply posed by unfavourable weather, disease or other factors that might lead to crop failure.

The loss of habitat cleared for farming purposes and the loss of knowledge and skills (such as hunting and gathering skills) meant that if crops failed it was very difficult to replace the lost food supply. From 1845 to 1849, the Irish potato famine led to one million deaths as a result of the mass potato crop failings on which their diet was dependent.[23] [24]

Increases in size don't necessarily translate into improvements in the quality of life for individuals. Larger societies generally lead to centralisation of power and a reduction in individual freedoms and liberties. Whether in a family, a tribe or a thriving metropolis, there are always decisions that need to be made which impact the broader group and which some members of the group are likely to be happier with than others, whatever the decision-making process. Decisions could be a question of what to hunt that day or whether a freeway runs past someone's house, but they could also be life or death decisions (either directly or indirectly). Where a conflict arises within a small group there is likely to be a bond between the affected parties either directly or through a third party. There is also likely to be one or several individuals who are respected by the affected parties and who can assist with mediating disagreements. The intimacy of the group also means that single parties are less likely to have a preferred outcome which seriously and negatively impacts another party. Within larger groups, family and friendship ties become less important and decision making becomes more difficult.

Larger group size is not always desirable and for the individual there may have been many reasons to avoid the transition from nomadic hunter-gatherer to sedentary farmer – but the choice wasn't always theirs to make. Like Richard Dawkins' "selfish gene", societies are not necessarily there to serve us as individuals or to help us achieve what we might define as a fulfilling and joyous life.[25] The society that adopted farming alongside a range of principles and customs that enabled it to grow in size and complexity over time had the capacity to absorb or destroy other societies which did not have these features. But those societies that did grow needed rules to function beyond those genetically hardwired into our brains.

Social Technologies

Our body of knowledge, processes and technologies have grown enormously thanks to the efforts of many brains in increasingly complex societies working together to come up with solutions to our problems. At the same time, our societies would never have reached the size and level of complexity that they have without the myriad of technologies that have enabled this growth. While many of these technologies are the kind that you can touch and feel, like the pipes in plumbing or the hardware of the internet, many equally or even more important social technologies cannot be seen or touched.

Social technologies have helped to address the problems involved with the transition to larger groups. The most basic development necessary in this transition is a process for making and enforcing decisions. Modern government, legislative, legal and justice systems, police and defence forces and all manner of public services represent and act on decisions that impact broader society. All of these technologies have evolved in size and complexity from much simpler beginnings as mechanisms for solving the problems that emerged as our societies grew beyond their natural limits.[26 27]

In smaller groups decisions would usually fall to one or more elders who are respected and probably have strong family ties within the group. Within larger groups individuals may not know the decision makers at all. Instead, it is necessary that they understand and have respect for the decision-making process as they are confronted by decisions, delivered by strangers, that could be placing the interest of someone they don't know or care about above their own. In effect, members of a society are balancing the benefit that they and their family receive from belonging to a larger group with the disadvantages or limitations that group membership may place on them, such as loss of autonomy or submission to an external authority. Conceptually, if the disadvantages outweigh the advantages we might want to leave, but it's not always easy to just up and live somewhere else. Even if we can leave there's very few places we could go where we would not be subject to someone else's rule – and there are also other reasons to stay.

Societies are an extension of our family or our tribe. They are part of our identity. Aside from the protective and economic benefits a larger society can provide, after eating and breathing, a sense of belonging is one of the most powerful human drivers. If we were to find ourselves alone, most of us would seek it out. We would give up a significant degree of personal freedom in order to belong to a group. We would like the society's laws and rules to reflect and help us achieve our individual desires but sometimes, because we wish to belong in the first place, we accept things that we otherwise would not.

Social technologies evolve under the influence of its members, but a society's priorities may be closely aligned or far removed from the priorities of its members. This might be because of the influence of a powerful subgroup but it could also be because social technologies evolve over hundreds or even thousands of years. Traditions, norms, culture and political infrastructure form under the stewardship of generations of caretakers each consciously or subconsciously adapting them to the challenges they face. Some adaptations may not be suited to dealing with subsequent times or challenges but become so ingrained in the social infrastructure that their influence can go unquestioned or even unnoticed.

Like genetic mutations, changes to social technologies that increase a society's chances of survival are likely to be retained and to propagate. Farming, for example, enabled a society to grow and influence, fend off, or even absorb other societies.

Economics

Farming facilitated by necessary developments in social technologies enabled more people to be fed from the same or a smaller area of land. This may have led to time savings which enabled individuals to engage in activities other than feeding themselves, including more free time. But the capacity to produce more had to be acted on, and not because they needed more to eat. When the growth of a society became a critical competitive factor, technologies that support and enhance growth also grew in importance. Societies that could produce excess beyond immediate needs provided the potential for excess production which could be used to support the society and its growth in various other ways.

We have been trading within our families and social groups since basically forever. The hunter-gatherer distinction is essentially a social contract in which both sides split their resources. Within family and tribal groups we work together in a myriad of different ways to protect and provide for the group. This cooperation is so deeply ingrained in us that it is almost offensive and simplistic to think of it as transactional, but at some level that's exactly what it is. Intra-family and tribal cooperation provided early humans with a foundation for trading beyond their immediate group. Trade between groups over distance may have even been around for as long as 300,000 years, as long or even longer than anatomically modern humans.[28] Obsidian, a preferred material for creating stone tools was being traded around the Mediterranean up to 10,000 years ago and in New Guinea across 800 kilometres of ocean from around 5,000 years ago.[29 30]

Trade permitted the exchange of goods and services across larger groups and ultimately between groups. It enabled farmers to concentrate on farming, increasing their output while other individuals, having displayed talent in certain areas, became dedicated to the tasks at which they had shown proficiency, allowing them to refine their skills and knowledge, to pass on that accumulated knowledge to others and to gradually increase the quantity and quality of the overall group's resources. Greater resources permit larger group sizes and the distribution of resources via trade permits more complex transactions or interactions. Trade between groups also enables us to inhabit and thrive in areas that might have an abundance of one resource but be deficient in another. This in turn releases new resources that may only be available in the new settlement area. The hunter-gatherer lifestyle gave us the foundations for trade, and it provided the foundation for another critical social/economic technology – the division of labour.

The term hunter-gatherer speaks traditionally to the split of tasks between men and women. Although it is not always the case – women also hunt and men also gather - there does appear to be preferences for both sexes likely related to the types of activities that were more or less conducive with breast-feeding and otherwise caring for infants and young children. This sexual division of labour enabled Homo sapiens to better utilise their collective resources and may actually have been one of the catalysts that ultimately saw humans take over from the Neanderthals as the most interesting species on the planet.[31 32]

When we focus on performing a particular task, we tend to get better at it. We also tend to figure out ways to improve our own performance of the task. Some gender differences were in place before the emergence of the hunter-gatherer split. In all primate species the males are bigger and generally physically stronger than the females and when it came to splitting tasks this was probably as good a reason as any for men to play a bigger role in hunting. Other characteristics appear to have emerged since we made this split. That men generally have better long-distance vision and women a better eye for detail over shorter distances appears to have evolved sometime after the hunter-gatherer distinction emerged.[33 34] Most improvements haven't become part of our genetic make-up, but within the course of our own lifetimes we are capable of developing an amazing aptitude for a huge range of tasks to which we might devote ourselves to.

An amazing aspect of task specialisation was outlined by economist David Ricardo. It is of course possible for one person to be better than others at more than one thing, and in a small community perhaps the best hunter is also the best butcher. Perhaps when he focuses all of his time on hunting his catch is 10% higher than the other hunters and maybe when he spends all of his time on butchery he is able to skin and divide 30% more carcasses than the other butchers. It may appear to make practical sense for him to divide his time between hunting and butchery. But David Ricardo demonstrated that the smartest thing for him to do is to concentrate his efforts on the activity in which he has the greatest advantage over his peers – in this case, butchery. His meagre yet enthusiastic fellows should concentrate on what they do best in comparison. They're not very good butchers, but they're not too bad on the hunt. When they try and divide their own carcasses they fumble around, curse a lot and leave a horrible mess. If they hand over their catch to the butcher, they can get straight back to doing what they (comparatively) do best while he makes light work of the cadaver. Comparative advantage, combined with trade and the division of labour, means that we can best solve our own problems by focusing on the things we are good at, and when we do that, we inadvertently help reduce other people's problems as well. [35] [36]

Economics is the science of using available resources efficiently. It is often referred to as the science of common sense. This is perhaps because many of the findings of economic theory suggest that we should continue doing things that we have often already been doing for thousands of years. This may not sound like much of a contribution, but it can be critically important when others are arguing that we should be doing something different. One common sense example is that individuals are best placed to decide what is right for them. This is not just a statement on liberty and individual freedoms; it is based on the fact that our social and economic systems are incredibly complex and unpredictable as they themselves are made up of many dynamic, reactive and unpredictable parts.[37][38]

Schools of fish have long been suspected of possessing some form of communication beyond our present understanding that enables them to move as a graceful, unified entity, but studies have shown that this is not the case. A giant school consisting of many thousands of individuals is able to give the appearance of a coordinated effort because every single fish concentrates on and reacts to the movement and behaviour of their immediate neighbours.[39] Human economies work in a similar way. There is no mystical voice that tells the many thousands of businesses in an economy what to produce, what to buy or how much to pay their staff. Instead, it is Adam Smith's invisible hand that sees a retail business reacting to the behaviours of its customers; if their customers buy out a particular item they need more of it, if there is another item customers don't want then they won't stock it again.[40][41] Wholesalers react to behaviours and to the orders coming in from the retailers, adjusting the orders that they themselves pass onto the manufacturers. Manufacturers adapt their production based on orders they receive, improving or developing new products and subsequently ordering more or less of the necessary raw materials. The whole time all participants adjust how many staff they need, what quality of coffee they can afford to put in the tearoom and where they should hold the office Christmas party this year. It is impossible for one person or central body to predict how an economy will react to certain changes; they do not have the level of information available to all the individual participants. They don't have the brainpower. No matter how smart one person or a central body could possibly be they are no match for the for the power of every brain in the community crunching the data they have immediately available to them to make their own decisions. They also don't have the motivation. Nobody cares more or puts more effort into solving our problems than we do.

Social technologies that facilitate cooperation and other economically advantageous practices help societies thrive.

Physical technologies

Social technologies pave and light the way for physical technologies – and vice versa. The concentration of larger numbers of people provides a fertile breeding ground for ideas, experimentation and the development of new physical technologies. The hoe, the scythe and irrigation channels enabled people to gather and work together in the first place.

Looking out the window at a thriving city, it's hard to

imagine the sheer number of improvements that have taken us from the first anatomically modern humans of approximately 100,000 years ago to the world that we live in today. Every man-made thing that we meet today was conceptualised as a brand-new thing, or merger of things at some point in history, then designed, carved, refined and re-designed to the thing we see today. Take the pen. Its foundation can be traced back to the sharp stone tools used to carve markings into cave walls, through to sticks dipped in a mix of fluids and ground minerals, styluses for marking wax covered tablets, feathers and pots of ink, fountain pens with their own inkwells, through to ball points and fluoro highlighters.[42] Each step was dependent on countless innovations and supporting innovations that facilitated the new instruments' use and production. Early humans would mine pigments and search for the best binding agents among their available resources, including animal fats, vegetable juice and bone marrow. Later wax tablets required the right mix of beeswax, oils and pigments for durability and ease of use. The quill pen required very precise selection and preparation of the feather and the right consistency of ink to ensure a balance between gravity and capillary action would keep it flowing at the preferred rate.[43] Modern, mass-produced ballpoint pens combine a hard durable plastic casing, a precision manufactured tungsten carbide ball-bearing, and a fraction of a millilitre of ink to provide an instrument capable of writing for kilometres at about 50 cents apiece.[44] There are probably hundreds of thousands – if not millions – of small developments and improvements contributed by nearly as many people or groups over thousands of years to make this possible. And just about every human-conceived item that we use on an average day has been through (and is still going through) a similar process.

Physical technologies are the concepts and designs that we can make real and use today, but we also benefit from the physical existence of capital stock that we use and benefit from every day. These include roads, bridges, plumbing systems, dams, aqueducts, utility networks, public transport systems, factories, ships and countless buildings and capital goods that we continue to benefit from long after they were built.

Physical technologies are one of the products of progress; they can make our lives easier, healthier, safer or more fun. But they are also facilitators and accelerators of progress. Everything we have comes from a mix of human and physical resources which then form the technological foundation for us and subsequent generations to build on, hopefully further improving our lives and the lives of our descendants.

Breakable

Today, many of us may have the luxury of assuming that this progress has emerged over thousands of years like a slowly rising tide, steady and unstoppable. Unfortunately, that's not how it has worked for most of humanity.

Physical technologies will remain in use if they add value and will be discarded if they don't. Their benefit is generally apparent across time and space and their advantages are sometimes, but not easily, lost. Our DNA is subject to rare and random mutations, which are gradually embedded into our DNA if they are beneficial and which disappear if they are not. Most social technologies are intangible, and their benefit open to interpretation. When we are dissatisfied with DNA, beyond exercise, diet, drugs and surgery there's not much we can do about it. To the extent that we might be dissatisfied with our society however, we can potentially bring about very significant and rapid change. Most genetic changes are slight with negative mutations impacting only the host. Societal mutations can be dramatic and have the potential to impact everyone.

Getting it wrong

China has a long history as a successful nation of farmers. Although not high by international standards their grain output in the 1950s was sufficient to feed the largest population in the world with enough left over to make them a net exporter.[45] In 1949, under the influence of the pleasant sounding and unproven theories of Karl Marx and Vladimir Lenin, Mao Zedong and the Chinese Communist Party set about abolishing private ownership and eliminating the capitalist class. Ownership of land was forbidden, and landlords and wealthy peasants were targeted, stripped of their holdings and often killed. Land holdings were initially grouped into communes and worked by an average of 170 families led by party officials.[46 47] Communist Party leadership was not content, however, and in 1958 the Party proclaimed the launch of a new movement, "the Great Leap Forward", which would supposedly propel the Chinese economy forward and enable it to surpass the industrial output of the United States within the next 30 years. Communes were increased to 20,000 to 30,000 workers each. Significant resources were shifted away from agriculture to industry and secondary production such as steel to push the nation towards wide-scale industrialisation. The reduction in resources available to the agricultural sector was expected to be compensated for by a range of measures expected to increase output. One measure was simply to demand more from workers. Output was to be redistributed to workers in the new industrial sectors at a set quota with agricultural workers required to survive on whatever was left over.[48 49 50]

Landholding farmers were previously incentivised to maximise the output of their farm as they directly benefited from their own efforts. Collectivisation and the transfer of quotas to industrial workers meant that farmers' individual efforts had little impact on how much they and their families would actually receive. Many of the measures designed to increase output also failed. Stalinist doctrine viewed every failure as stemming from a class-war. It was believed that plants of the same variety would not compete with each other and could therefore be planted together in densities that experienced farmers would never have attempted. With so much effort going into industrialisation there was little capacity to bring improvements to agriculture that would have really made a difference – like fertiliser and modern equipment. When Mao Zedong visited a commune to check on farming conditions, starving peasants were ordered to uproot and replant thousands of grain-stalks into a single field which was displayed to Mao as proof of the programme's success.[50 51]

As production efficiency fell, so did consumption efficiency with the introduction of an additional innovation – communal dining. Private kitchens were banned, and pots and pans melted down to contribute to the industrialisation effort. It was perceived that home-cooking was a waste of human resources that could be applied to helping the collective. Workers would eat in communal dining halls. They were encouraged to eat as much as they wanted, which was often more than they needed and which, when combined with mass food production, led to a degree of wastage not seen in private kitchens. It removed the natural incentives for individuals to maximise their output, as the amount of food received in the dining halls was in no way related to the amount of work they did during the day. It also removed personal incentive to control consumption as the amount eaten one day would not impact the amount of food available to them the next.[50]

By the end of 1958 food shortages and starvation were being reported in some areas. Local communist party officials eager to meet the difficult quotas they had been set exaggerated the output of communes and transferred more grain to urban areas than they could afford, leaving their own workers to go hungry. Initial reductions in output meant that the already reduced number of agricultural workers did not have enough to eat and could not work as hard (farmers were starving at twice the rate of other workers) and output fell further.[51 52]

The results were catastrophic. By the end of the Great Leap Forward in 1962, Chinese grain production had fallen by 30% and up to 45 million people had died. It is perhaps the greatest loss of life in all human history. The tragedy was no doubt exacerbated by drought and difficult climatic conditions, but the greater part of the blame undoubtedly lies with these and similar government policies of the time. several studies have suggested that perhaps 60-70% of the blame lies with the government's policies and management efforts. Eventually, having somewhat admitted to the failure of its policies, the Chinese government permitted the import of grain towards the end of 1962. Small plots of land were returned to the workers and people were allowed to return to their own kitchens. The famine subsequently ended within six months.[51 52 53]

China has a 4000-year history of agriculture. Although the industrial revolution meant that many western nations had recently reached a level of development significantly beyond that of the Chinese, China was level pegging with European nations in terms of overall output up until the late 1800s.[54] [55] While the Communist Party's policies probably looked like a nice idea on paper, many of its policies either totally ignored or underestimated the many fundamental human and social factors which had been sustaining the world's largest society. They withdrew the individual's capacity to control his or her own outcome and they removed all links between an individual's efforts and their rewards. In trying to coordinate the Chinese people towards achieving a particular outcome efficiently, they distorted those very decisions that give economies the appearance of coordination and which by their nature deliver efficiency.

Flexible and dynamic social structures have helped to deliver much of the prosperity that we enjoy today. Their distortion and manipulation permitted Mao Zedong and the Chinese Communist Party to implement changes that resulted in the deaths of up to 45 million people.

Delicate balance

We wake up hungry and we strive every day to survive and come up with ways to make it easier for us to survive the following day. We form groups which in turn fight for their own continued existence and have grown very large and complex in the process. Both these battles, over thousands of years, have forged a massive body of knowledge, processes, social and physical technologies, which have led us to the privileged position in which much of humanity finds itself today.

However, this human growth machine is not infallible or uninterruptible. Of the contributing factors it is only our hunger and our mental capacity that are stable and guaranteed to function pretty much the same wherever we go, as long as we exist. Society and the social and physical technologies that leverage our individual capacities can vary dramatically.

Hopefully, they improve over time in a manner that increases that leverage to a greater and greater extent. Today the average wage earner in a developed country needs to work about 15 to 30 minutes to afford a Big Mac.[56] Such a level of prosperity is incredibly precious, but also fragile. Most of our social technologies are not hard-wired. They are intangible and subject to misunderstanding, neglect or outright abuse. The example provided above is only one of many occasions throughout human history where manipulation of our social technologies has proven disastrous for a society's members. There are countless other examples in which these technologies and the institutions they facilitate have hampered our progress in less dramatic, yet still damaging, ways. Our understanding and vigilance is required to hinder such tragedies and ensure that the economy continues to work for us to deliver real, positive developments into our lives.

CHAPTER THREE

FAITH

The people still standing in the aftermath of a zombie apocalypse are usually the pragmatic, multiskilled types, coming from either the military or a variety of trades. The white-collar workers, the university professors, database programmers and investment bankers all tend to get picked off pretty early. This is probably a reasonable assumption. Surviving on your own in a challenging environment requires a range of practical skills like obtaining water and food, securing your home, building weapons, defending yourself, hot-wiring cars and so on. Having an in-depth understanding of a very specific field is less likely to be helpful – and yet in our modern world, we are surrounded by such individuals. We have a specialist for every area of expertise and the jack-of-all-trades is often less highly valued than those individuals who have dedicated great portions of their lives to becoming very knowledgeable and very skilled in just one thing.

The factors detailed in the previous chapter were essential to the formation of a system within which such specialists are available to help us solve an immense range of problems. However, there is one additional factor, like the fire pumping heated air into the balloon, which is integral to keeping the whole thing aloft: faith. Faith is everywhere in economics – or at least, it is needed everywhere.

The Specialist

When we divide tasks among best suited individuals, we increase overall output. Individuals become better at the tasks at which they concentrate, as they can seek out focused training and invest more time and resources in developing or acquiring tools and processes to further increase their output. They can meet with other experts to further expand their knowledge and they can position themselves in the most suitable location for their activity. Whatever their field of expertise might be, however, it won't be the only thing that they need to survive. For an individual to choose specialisation over generalisation, they must believe that their strategy will work in their favour. They can only concentrate their efforts on doing what they do best when they have faith that they can exchange their own output for all the other elements essential for their own survival. During the COVID 19 pandemic of 2020, social distancing and lockdowns slowed or shuttered large sections of the economy and triggered panic buying of essential goods. The pandemic was a sudden reminder that as modern humans we are not well equipped to provide for our own needs. Instead, we are fed, clothed, sheltered and supported by an economy that facilitates and depends on other people. If we don't have confidence in this economy, or that our needs can be provided for, then we have no choice but to generalise. Individuals or small groups must find a way to provide for their own needs, removing the benefits of specialisation and drastically reducing the amount, quality and diversity of the goods and services available to everyone.

To risk specialisation means that we must have faith in the economy, but it also means that we must have faith in our society, that we and our possessions are safe and that the product of our specialisation belongs to us. That automatically extends to what we might receive in exchange for the goods and services that we produce, because those things are the reason that we produce in the first place. If we don't feel that our lives and property are protected, then there is less reason to produce in the first place and we would need to focus more of our thoughts and efforts on meeting our basic needs – we would have to generalise. Like the San, for whom there is no reason to produce or possess more than what they can carry, there is no reason for us to produce more than what we can protect or retain.

We also need to believe that the system within which we

are operating is relatively stable. We might feel safe today, but if we think that situation could change at any time then we will not be able to devote ourselves to a single activity. We will also be less likely to make investments in the future. Developmental economists, Ariel BenYishay and Sarah Pearlman, have shown that one of the key causes of micro businesses in Mexico choosing not to invest is simply the (in many cases) realistic concern that their investment would be stolen. Support programmes may focus on helping small entrepreneurs improve their business practices or provide access to credit, but business owners are understandably less likely to invest if there is a strong chance that their investment will be taken away from them.[1] BenYishay and Pearlman also provided evidence to suggest that violent crime reduces the number of hours people work. Specifically, in one study a 10 per 100,000 increase in homicide rates reduced hours worked by 1%, with people in high homicide areas more likely to want to go home before it gets dark.[2][3] Our personal safety and the security of our belongings are essential. We might know that we can be of much more value and make a lot more money if we spend five years at university or buy a particularly expensive piece of equipment or even working later into the night, but we will not do those things if we don't feel that we are safe, now and for a sufficiently long period into the future.

Many of the functions critical to our sense of security and stability are outsourced to our governments. Governments coordinate legal systems, police forces, national defence and usually most health-care systems. The less faith we have in our governments to address these issues, the more effort we need to put into meeting these needs ourselves. This is not to suggest that we are not responsible for our own safety and wellbeing. We choose what to eat and what streets to walk down late at night, but if we live in an environment in which we feel safe we are able to focus our efforts on the things we do best, enabling us to make our biggest contribution while others can focus on what they do best, resulting in more and higher quality resources overall.

This faith is so central to developed nations that it rarely receives a second thought. It is fundamental to the many small (if sometimes obscure) contributions that collectively enable modern economies to produce a phenomenal range and quantity of goods and services in the most part, incredibly efficiently. Job titles mean relatively little in today's economy, a "teacher" can spend their entire time designing learning aids, a "fireman" might spend his time standing in front of a classroom teaching children how to prevent and put out fires. Contributions are sometimes very obscure. There are individuals who know how to repair machines that build other machines. There are people who examine the sound waves emitted by nuclear reactors to minimise the damage caused by the resulting vibrations. There are people who study the behaviours and migratory patterns of animals and advise strategies such as fencing, land bridges or relocation programmes to offset the impact caused by new freeways or developments on population levels. There are people standing by to wash our dogs, spray on tans or advise us how to rearrange our closets. Modern economies support and are supported by the widest, sometimes weirdest, and most wonderful array of professions.

Of the many thousands – if not millions – of professions in existence today, some are more and some are less valuable than others, and it's tough to tell which one's which. The free-market system means that those who engage the services or buy the goods are the ones who decide its value.[4] We all have experience of farmers, teachers and nurses, and can readily ascribe a value to their services. We don't necessarily have experience with database programmers, French history professors or nuclear technicians/sound engineers. They are paid for their services by someone who receives a direct value from them, or because it enables those people to provide a service better or cheaper to someone else (and hence receive more in exchange for their own efforts). In a highly advanced economy, the contributions can become more obscure – not just because we have more money to spend, but because competition forces businesses to look for any possible method of improving efficiency and output. Reducing wastage of raw materials, employee absences or production times, or increasing brand loyalty, crop yield or any of a million other contributing factors can make the difference between a business's success or failure. And all the well- and little-known areas of expertise each contribute in their own way to these different factors. Individuals may make a millimetre of difference, but those millimetres accumulate and combine to see our economies deliver such consistent high return for the effort required that even the San tribes people might have sufficient cause to feel a little bit jealous.

Supply and Demand

Our faith is strong, but it is not blind. Global pandemics, financial crises, or even speeding fines may cause us to begin to worry about our financial well-being. Depending on how worried we are we might decide to reduce our spending. We might start by cutting down on luxury items, discretionary goods and services, those things that we don't desperately need. Some cost cutting might not mean much. But some reductions may also have had real value, they might have been contributing in a small way to our own and perhaps the economy's efficiency, and/or to our own well-being.[5 6]

Regardless of how important those goods and services may be to the people buying them, they are incredibly valuable to the people selling them. If the suppliers weren't already worried about the stability of their incomes, for the same reasons as their customers, they soon will be when their customers stop buying their goods. Businesses too, then look to cut costs. The most significant cost most businesses face is labour, so business may directly reduce staff.[7 8 9] Even if they retain their staff and reduce costs in other areas, it means that another business is making less money and they in turn perhaps may need to reduce their staff.

This can occur without any initial reduction in the amount produced. One day everyone's working hard producing at their maximum capacity, the next day due to a fall in confidence individuals reduce their spending. A small farmer who produces 100 kilos of vegetables might need 10 kilos to feed his family. If confident they will be able to produce an additional 100 kilos the following week, they will have 90 kilos of excess vegetables that they could choose to exchange for some new clothes or tools (to help increase output). If the person who sells them the tools or the clothes shares the farmer's confidence, they too will keep just 10 kilos of vegetables and exchange the remaining 80 kilos for something else. In this way the 100 kilos of vegetables can be distributed through the economy, feeding 10 families in exchange for a range of goods and services. It enables the people who make clothes and tools to contribute their efforts to the economy rather than spending time growing their own vegetables. The 100 kilos of vegetables therefore generates 100 kilos of efficient, specialised economic activity, with each person keeping enough vegetables for themselves before passing the rest on in exchange for something else.

But a small reduction in confidence that causes each participant to think that maybe they should hold onto 2 weeks supply of vegetables means that only five families will be fed for that week, and fewer clothes and tools will be bought and sold. The clothing and the tools makers must try to get by with less, to raid their own stores if they have them, and perhaps to drop the price of their goods. If no one is buying their goods or is only willing to buy them at a price that is unprofitable to the supplier then the clothing and tools makers may need to divert their activities to something else, possibly to producing more food. In this way a small reduction in confidence can lead to a reduction in demand which can impact supply and reduce overall output and efficiency of the economy.[10]

In a 2015 study, Jonathan Heathcote and Fabrizio Perri demonstrated that fear of an economic downturn can be self-fulfilling. For example, if people expect unemployment to increase, they may increase their savings and reduce their spending – which subsequently reduces economic activity and leads employers to lay-off workers, ultimately increasing unemployment as initially feared. They found that this effect is magnified when wealth levels are low. This is because people have less resources to call upon and are more likely to increase savings if they are worried about their jobs. Where wealth levels are high people are less concerned about possible unemployment, leading them to maintain their spending which in turn helps to maintain employment levels.[11]

There are a number of variables which can limit or exacerbate the impact of falling confidence. When faced with reduced demand, suppliers may reduce their prices.

Lower prices make goods and services more attractive to buyers and may by themselves be sufficient to reignite demand. But in a competitive environment suppliers might not have much scope to lower prices before they begin losing money. They may not be able to lower prices to the extent that consumers would be motivated to increase their spending.

The sectors most likely to remain afloat in a downturn supply the things that we can't do without, such as food and housing. We might quickly reduce our discretionary spending on things like travel and entertainment, but will be more resistant to reducing spending on essential items. There are also many practical realities to most people's incomes that influence how a downturn plays out. A large portion of the population will be employed on a permanent or contract basis and reducing staff numbers comes with significant up-front costs that businesses would prefer to avoid. Developed economies also have a long history of business cycles, of expansions and contractions. Individuals and firms do not expect downturns to be catastrophic. They expect incomes to eventually be restored. They have worked hard to reach the pre-downturn levels of output and they would often prefer to see their profits or savings drop and to be ready for the recovery than to drastically cut their costs. Neither businesses nor individuals can change tack and grow enough vegetables in a day or a week to feed themselves (even if they still know how). Much of a business's revenues and costs are often also more or less contractually secured. Businesses are committed to supplying their customers and their customers are committed to paying for goods and services. Businesses are usually locked into multi-year leases, multi-year loans and multiple supply and purchase contracts. It's not just a matter of switching off the lights and closing the door behind them. Of course, if things get really bad then businesses and individuals can default on their obligations, but this usually comes with significant consequences that people will work hard to try and avoid.

When workers in developed nations lose their jobs, they are not usually immediately destitute and out on the street. In addition to whatever personal savings they already have, they may get a pay-out from their former employer and/or they may be entitled to some form of ongoing support from the government or an insurance provider. Progressive income tax then means that if people end up earning less money either because their hours are reduced or they are forced into a lower paying job, they will usually also end up paying less tax both in real dollar terms and a lower percentage of their overall income.[12] Governments also tend to maintain or even increase spending when private sector activity falls and central banks reduce interest rates and the interest expense of borrowing and spending money. In response to the Global Financial Crisis of 2008 and to the Covid 19 crisis of 2020 governments dramatically increased their spending and debt levels, while central banks lowered interest rates and instigated massive asset buying programs to maintain the flow of money in the economy.[13 14 15]

These factors have an impact on economic activity, but importantly they also have an impact on confidence. Heathcote and Perri saw unemployment benefits as one of the key factors in reducing confidence-linked downturns, and countries that had the lowest unemployment benefits suffered some of the largest increases in unemployment during the Covid 19 crisis.[11 16] Even those countries with traditionally low unemployment benefits such as the US significantly increased benefit payments during the pandemic in an effort to mitigate further impacts to demand.

Money

The complex marketplace created by specialisation goes way beyond the limited range of goods and services that can be sensibly traded. It makes much more sense for the specialist to receive money for their services and then to use that money to buy the specific amount of goods or services that he or she desires. Money plays a very big role in our economies but ultimately, it's there because life is way too complicated to get much done without it.

Money is another feature of modern economics that is totally dependent on faith.[17 18] The moment that we exchange something of ours (whether goods or services) for something other than what it is that we really want (such as for money instead of food) there is a risk that one or a couple of things could go wrong. When we go to exchange the money for food, there might not be any food available. The people selling the food might not accept our money. When we want to buy the food, our money might be worth less to the people selling the food than we thought it would and we might end up with less food than we expected.

A lack of faith in money can have similar consequences to a lack of faith in the economy. To focus on our specialties, we need to be able to convert our efforts into something tangible and exchangeable that we are confident we can trade for the many other things that we might need. Otherwise, we would be forced to reduce the amount and complexity of our transactions, which would reduce the total value of our output. Rice, for example, carries a lot of similar characteristics to money. But it is ultimately perishable and it is very heavy, meaning you'd need a lot of it to trade for anything of significant value. But we can't eat money. For us to accept money as payment we need to have as much faith in our ability to convert money into something edible as we do in being able to eat the rice.

The financial system

Most money sits in bank accounts, term deposits, government bonds, pension funds, shares and other investments. From there it is usually used for something. It is lent or invested via credit cards, loans, mortgages and capital raisings allowing people, businesses and governments to buy items they otherwise might not be able to afford; a dress, a house, a new manufacturing plant or a bridge over a river. On one side of the equation an individual or institution has more money than they need at that point in time and on the other side of the equation a firm or individual has less than what they need at that moment but has the capacity to pay the money back in the future with interest. This process is incredibly important to the functionality of the modern economy.

An effective financial system matches people who have more money than they need with people who have less, in a way that ideally keeps both happy.[19 20] In the process it should also hopefully address one of the key issues outlined earlier. When individuals and firms become concerned about the stability of their incomes, they are likely to increase their savings. While that means they are reducing the amount of money that they are spending and the amount of goods and services they are buying, it also increases the amount of money that is available for people who need and want to spend it. This can work if one sector of the economy is experiencing difficult times as other sectors remain strong. The money flows from an area in which savings are higher than spending or investment, to another area where spending or investment is higher than saving.

But for the financial system to provide these benefits, just as people need to have faith in each other, in the economy and in money, they also need to have faith in the financial system. If people don't trust banks or the companies, they might consider lending to or investing in, they will hold back the value of their excess output, either as cash or as something tangible like gold or extra food in the cupboard. This can be the case in developing nations where there is often less confidence in banks and financial institutions than in those of developed nations. Historically, Argentina has suffered many economic and financial crises – including defaulting on its sovereign debt nine times since the nineteenth century.[21] [22] Argentinians do not have a lot of faith in their currency or in their financial institutions as they continue to suffer through bouts of high inflation and economic instability. Under an agreement with the International Monetary Fund (IMF), Argentina is attempting to increase its foreign currency reserves, but this is proving difficult with reserves falling recently and currently sitting at approximately US$32 billion.[23] By contrast, it is estimated that Argentinians have eight times that amount, or about US$250 billion, sitting in overseas bank accounts, safety deposit boxes or in their homes.[24] The Argentinian people's understandable lack of faith in their nation's financial system means that Argentinian companies, governments, and the Argentinians themselves miss out on the potential benefits such an amount could provide if it were invested into the Argentinian economy. Faith in the financial system also helps an economy's capacity to be used and used efficiently.

Too much of a good thing

As anyone who's hit the dance floor drunk on a Friday night can tell you, it's definitely possible to have too much confidence. Just like alcohol, confidence is a variable input. When there's plenty of it to go around, everything is fabulous and all sorts of crazy behaviour seems perfectly okay. But the next morning when the pleasant, feel-good effects subside, we can be left with a very unpleasant hangover. In an economic sense, high levels of confidence may not see people dancing on the bar and hooking up with random strangers (though it probably causes a bit of that too), but it does lead to all sorts of behaviours which could be considered risky and inappropriate from a sober perspective. When markets are flush with confidence people will spend more than what they might otherwise, and they will often borrow and spend even more.[25] They are less likely to be concerned with saving money, confident in the belief that it shouldn't be too hard to get more of it. Demand for goods and services may be very high as people choose to spend amounts of money on things they otherwise wouldn't. The peak of the business cycle is renowned for its excess. This could result in van Goghs for the price of a hospital wing, but it could also impact the behaviour of regular consumers and regular businesses.

The US auto manufacturers, Ford, General Motors and Chrysler, have struggled to remain competitive against their international rivals for the last few decades. These big three US producers have suffered from the high costs of a highly unionised US labour force who enjoy pensions and other benefits far in excess of even other US employees of foreign-owned manufacturers. They have also failed to keep pace with consumer demands and have struggled to profitably produce small to midsize vehicles. In the late 1990s, strong economic conditions held up demand for the more profitable, inefficient larger car and SUV segment. Consumers were confident enough to keep buying SUVs, US producers were confident enough to continue ignoring their high labour costs and lack of a competitive offering in the smaller, more fuel-efficient categories. As a result of a recession that began in 2000, SUV sales peaked in 1999 and US producer sales and profits began to decline. In 2005 oil prices began to increase steeply, peaking in 2008. Consumers still otherwise drawn to inefficient SUVs began to place more emphasis on the fuel efficiency for which other manufacturers were renowned. In 2008 the global financial crisis also hit. Consumers who had previously been using lines of credit supported by increasing house prices were either no longer able or no longer willing to further increase their indebtedness to continue buying uneconomical vehicles. The crisis also impacted the US producers' access to credit and their very existence was under threat. In November 2008 the CEOs of General Motors, Ford and Chrysler flew to Washington DC in their company jets to ask for financial assistance. GM and Chrysler ultimately received close to US$100 billion in taxpayer funded assistance. GM filed for bankruptcy protection in June 2009.[26] [27] [28] [29]

The businesses that fail during recessions may have been operating on the edge of consumers wants and desires, but they may also have been less competitive than other suppliers. Perhaps an economic downturn has led some suppliers to lower prices – and while some had margins or balance sheets fat enough to handle the contraction, others may have ended up producing at a loss and been forced out of business. Others may have been providing services in an area of specialisation upon which spending is easily reduced, such as advertising. This doesn't mean that some of these businesses and expenditures are not very important. In economic downturns two of the sectors to see significant cutbacks, particularly within larger businesses, are marketing and research and development.[30] This might make sense in terms of senior management surviving the next reporting period, but it is these activities which often lend a business and an economy its millimetres of competitive advantage over the medium- to long-term, even during economic contractions.[31] US auto manufacturers were already struggling to keep pace with their competitors in these areas. They were not producing competitively, they were not producing vehicles that the public wanted, they had not kept up with competitors' product developments, particularly in terms of fuel efficiency. As a result, their balance sheets were already a mess before things got tough.

Other businesses produce great products and services very competitively but are simply more at the mercy of consumer whims. We can get by without fine dining, five-star hotels, art, jewellery, Megadeth concerts and Monster-Truck rallies, but life becomes a lot less entertaining. And more importantly (in the short term at least), all these products and services are sucking money out from under people's mattresses, keeping it in circulation and helping to keep the economy in motion.

Over the medium- to long-term, economic contractions help to keep economies, businesses and balance sheets fit, healthy and competitive.[32] Downturns force uncompetitive firms out of business. They force already competitive firms to become more so, to reduce costs, to figure out better, cheaper ways of doing things. They force individuals to consider their own preparedness, but they also often force individuals to shift from declining industries to those where their skills may be of more value. They force both individuals and businesses to think very hard about their expenses, their debt levels, how much money they have in the bank and whether it is sufficient to provide for the newly uncertain world. As confidence in their economy and in their own financial situation returns, people begin to take on more risk, growth returns and eventually memories of former downturns begin to fade. The very fact that individuals and firms strengthened their financial positions as a result of the previous downturn contributes to their growing confidence in the new upturn. Individuals and businesses begin to increase spending and reduce savings, taking on more debt and more risk. Eventually something, somewhere, dents people's confidence again and they reflect on their own readiness for a downturn; if they are not happy with what they find, if their growing confidence has resulted in low savings and their expenses, debts and risk being too high, then they will have more reason to fear.

The extent of this fear could (like most fears) be vaguely calculated as a factor of the danger posed by the external threat and the extent of personal readiness. If the external threat is moderate but we are ready, or if we are not ready but the threat is low, then there's probably not too much to worry about. If the external threat is high and our own readiness low, then there may be cause for panic. Fear then causes the downturn, but it also improves economic fitness and lays the foundations for the following recovery – which will increase confidence, exuberance, risk-taking and eventually increase the likelihood of another downturn.

While fear can sharpen the economy in the short run, faith is the air an economy breathes.[33] The people of Argentina have had their faith tested to the point that it is seriously diminished and will require a long period of economic and financial stability to get it back. Without faith in each other, in markets, in money and in the financial system, there would be no economy. Our faith in these things has accumulated and strengthened over a very long period – to the point that in most developed countries it is largely taken for granted. But this does not reduce its importance. If we lose our faith in our economy, we will have a different kind of apocalypse to contend with.

CHAPTER FOUR

THE MACHINES

Isaac Asimov's laws of robotics were guiding principles for his fictional robots.[1] They were Asimov's logical response to the Frankenstein complex, the idea that humanity's creations could turn against their creators.[2] The smart creator would know the risk of this happening and surely do something to prevent it. Even though they were his laws, much of Asimov's writing was focused on how they could fail or be circumvented. For example, the first law was, "A robot may not injure a human being or, through inaction, allow a human being to come to harm."[1] But if a robot sees one human about to harm another and the only way they can stop it from happening is to hurt the aggressor, then in adhering to the first part of the law they will break the second part and vice versa. The fourth law, the Zeroth law, was intended to precede all others and stated, "A robot may not harm humanity, or, by inaction, allow humanity to come to harm."[1] It is this law that VIKI, the supercomputer from "I, Robot", is trying to adhere to when, having decided it is the only way to protect humanity from itself, it tries to take control of everything.[3]

Under the influence of our constant, conscious efforts our tools have evolved into miraculously complex things that support our existence in a myriad of ways. It is a role that they perform diligently and without demand and it would be really unsettling if they one day grew smarter and more powerful than us and decided to take over – but in some ways, this has already happened.

Long before we developed physical technologies to do math, build cars or vacuum the floor, we had another form of technology that was also designed to help us achieve goals or complete tasks that were much more difficult without them. These technologies are the institutions that emerge from human desires and which are an extension of our own physical and social selves – but which have also taken on a life and momentum all their own. They consist of human and physical components such as offices, computers, machinery, vehicles, factories, equipment, forklifts and even robots of their own, all wrapped up in processes, customs, by-laws, constitutions, acts of parliament, books of worship, trust deeds, articles of incorporation, policies and procedures, but also in unwritten rules, cultural norms and codes of conduct.

We don't know when institutions beyond family and tribal groups first began to emerge, but they likely began to advance considerably approximately 10,000 years ago, at the conclusion of the last ice age and around the time farming communities sprung up throughout the Middle East. Religion likely predated other more deliberate governance structures, with shared customs and beliefs increasing the likelihood of cooperation between unrelated groups. Some of the earliest projects dependent on cooperation from larger groups were likely large scale irrigation projects supporting farming activity. Beginning in approximately 3500 BCE, Sumerians built and maintained an irrigation and agricultural system capable of supporting 20 city states including Uruk, the world's first city, which at its height had a population of up to 80,000 people. The unification of Upper and Lower Egypt and the formation of the First Dynasty in 3150 BCE then established a human society that would grow to approximately 3 million people under the rule of a single king, and which would exist as a single, independent nation for nearly 3000 years.[4 5]

Institutions exist to help us do things that individuals alone are not capable of, either because the task is too large or complex or because a more-than-human level of dedication, cooperation or consistency is required. What results is something that consists of human components and which is capable of things we alone cannot do. It took about 25,000 people over 20 years to build the Pyramid of Giza.[6] An army can stand guard 24 hours a day for a hundred years. A court of law can ensure people are judged equally and without prejudice. A hospital can provide round the clock care for a stranger in a way that not even their own family could replicate. The Ford Motor Company is 117 years old, it employs about 200,000 people and produces about 4 to million cars per year. It has helped literally billions of people get where they want to go.[7] [8] Institutions can also be less than human. They can separate individuals from the consequences of their actions, relieve them of their sense of personal responsibility and reward them for behaviours they might otherwise avoid. An army can kill with inhuman coldness and efficiency. A court can unjustly deprive a person of their freedom or choose to end a life without remorse. Tobacco companies can knowingly condemn swathes of a generation to crippling disease and early death with psychopathic detachment. Institutions can enhance our strengths and our weaknesses; they can go beyond the selflessness, selfishness, cruelty and kindness that is expected from raw humanity.

The concentration of power

For an institution to be able to do any of these things it has to be invested with a degree of power. Power, for example, to make and to act on decisions. Before an institution comes into existence it has nothing. An institution's power and capacity to achieve anything are lent to it by real people, people who have some degree of political, physical or economic power to begin with. A lobby group, a street gang or a small business can then quickly grow to have more political, physical or economic power than its contributors.

As more people invest in the institution, more people have an interest in its activities and more voices seek to direct those activities in their own preferred direction. If participants don't have a say in the direction of an institution, or if they aren't sufficiently rewarded by it, they won't support its development to begin with. But if we want an institution to become more than us, we end up having to forego some control over its direction.

The concentration of power in an institution leads to the creation of something else that we also have less control over. Steve Jobs founded Apple with Steve Wozniak but needed money for the company to become more than just two guys in a garage. Jobs and Wozniak could only attract investors such as Mike Markkula to the business if they were willing to give up some degree of control. In 1977 Markkula invested $250,000 for a 30% stake in the business. Markkula helped Apple to become more than what it was, but it also meant a dilution in control for the original owners. In 1985 Markkula, as Vice-Chairman of the Apple board, was central in the decision to sack Jobs from Apple.[9] [10]

A short time later, Jobs was travelling in the Soviet Union, and against the recommendation of his KGB escort, he delivered a speech praising Leon Trotsky. [11] Trotsky was a student of Vladimir Lenin, a compatriot of Joseph Stalin and central figure in the Russian revolution. Six years after having played a significant role in the formation of the Communist Party and the Soviet Union, Trotsky was exiled from the nation he had helped to create. [12] Both Jobs and Trotsky gave a substantial part of themselves to the formation of institutions which were capable of more than they could ever be as individuals, but which they also ultimately couldn't control. This similarity was presumably not the point of Jobs' speech.

Jobs famously later returned to Apple, helping to transform it into the biggest company in the world. Trotsky, though initially luckier than many of his contemporaries who were tortured and executed, was eventually tracked to his new home in Mexico and died shortly after being struck in the head with an ice axe wielded by an undercover Soviet agent.[13]

We must invest power into institutions in order for them to achieve their intended purpose. They can have physical power in the case of police or armed forces, they can have economic power in the case of a large company or bank, or they can have political power in the case of a government or bureaucracy. They often have all three. They can provide many benefits to the people that they are intended to serve. But once they have power to act, they can also act in ways that we may not have intended or don't like.

Make it or take it

The human growth machine is fuelled by individuals demanding better solutions to their problems and by rewarding those able to develop and deliver those solutions. However, this can be very hard and monotonous work. There is the daily grind of planting, tending, harvesting, designing, producing, baking, building whatever it is you deliver into the system to extract what you need for yourself. It can also be very risky. You must invest time, effort and significant money in order to refine your craft, profession, product or service, and then hope that whatever you produce is valuable enough that you will be able to acquire what you want in exchange. At the same time, depending on what it is you do, there might be a lot of people also trying to assist others in solving a similar problem. If all goes terribly, then you and your family may be dependent on the charity of others and will be very unlikely to achieve any of your more ambitious goals or (depending on your point in history) even to survive at all.

If you believe it's simply too hard to do the work yourself, if the rewards are not sufficient, the risks too great or perhaps if you're just stronger than you are industrious, the other option is to try and take what you want through the exercise of economic, political or physical power. We might prefer to think that we would not take advantage of others to satisfy our own desires, and while we may have evolved some emotional mechanisms that help us to work together and which cause a degree of conflict when responsible for the suffering of others, our fears and our desires are often stronger than our moral convictions. To get what we want, many of us will intrude on the freedoms of others. If our need is urgent enough, we will use whatever means we have at our disposal within the widely variable bounds of each individual's moral code. This is why institutions emerge in the first place. They are part of our arsenal; they protect us from threats and help us to achieve our goals. But as the power shifts from individuals and becomes concentrated in the machine of institutions, the most powerful position to be in, the best way to ensure you can achieve your goals, is to take control of the machine.

Francisco Macías Nguema was democratically elected as head of post-independence Equatorial Guinea in 1968. Although initially elected under a constitution requiring regular democratic elections, Nguema took absolute control of the government and declared himself "President for Life". Offending Nguema or his government could result in up to 30 years in prison, while threats to the president were punishable by death. Torture and executions were an everyday part of his rule. At Christmas 1975, he had 150 of his opponents rounded up and brought to a football stadium. "Those were the days" played over the stadium's loudspeakers as all 150 were executed.[14 15]

Today, Equatorial Guinea is led by Nguema's nephew,

Teodoro Obiang Nguema Mbasogo, Africa's longest standing leader. Forbes magazine has estimated that Obiang is worth approximately US$600 million – making him one of the world's wealthiest heads of state. [17] In 2003 he took US$500 million from the state treasury, deposited it in accounts controlled by himself and his family, telling his people it was necessary to prevent embezzlement by government employees.[18] [19] [20] In 2009 his son and Minister for Agriculture, Teodorin Obiang, drew up plans for what would have been the world's second largest private superyacht – worth approximately US$380 million, or nearly three times the country's combined health and education budget. The yacht was not built but Obiang and his family have been involved in other excesses.[21] In 2011 French police seized 11 supercars worth approximately US$5 million that belonged to Obiang and were held at his Paris residences.[22]

Equatorial Guinea has the highest per capita Gross Domestic Product (GDP) in sub-Saharan Africa and the twentieth highest in the world, however, it is also one of the worst ranked countries in the world in terms of income equality.[23] This is largely due to the existence of massive oil and gas reserves contrasted against a population of approximately 1.4 million people, and the concentration of the country's wealth around Obiang and his chosen elite. The country ranks 145th out of 189 countries on the United Nations Human Development Index. Approximately 70% of the population live in poverty and less than half have access to clean drinking water.[24 25]

Obiang came to power in 1979 through a bloody coup which ended with the execution of his uncle, former President for Life, Francisco Macías Nguema.[26] Obiang has won the last 5 national elections with approximately 98% of the vote on each occasion. In 2002, in one region of the country he received 103% of the vote.[27 28]

1 plus 1

A society is the sum of the individual and cooperative actions of its members. Those actions emerge as a consequence of individuals seeking to fulfil their desires within the constraints imposed on them by the institutions with which they live.

To maintain his grip on power, Francisco Nguema went to various extremes beyond mass executions. Hc banned fishing and had all boats burned to stop people fleeing the country.[26] The one road out of the country was peppered with landmines.[29] He was also so suspicious of intellectuals he had the word "intellectuals" banned.[30 31] Private education was also banned and simply possessing a page of written text could result in suspicion and possible punishment.[32]

Although ostensibly adhering to a different ideology, the North Korean government is equally controlling of its people. Nearly all property belongs to the state and there is no judicial system interested in protecting an individual's right of ownership. All official economic activity is directed by the government.[33] North Korea's economy had begun to improve in years prior to 2009 as individuals increased their participation in black market activities that drew additional income from cottage farming, handicrafts and other forms of business. It is estimated that 80% of the average person's income of approximately US$15 per month was drawn from these illegal activities with the remainder coming from their official, government designated roles.[34] [35] [36] [37] In 2009 the North Korean government decided to make some adjustments to the local currency, the won.[38] North Koreans were given one week during which they could exchange "old wons" for "new wons". The exchange rate was 100 old for every 1 new won. Similar exchanges have been undertaken in many countries before and the net result does not necessarily have to change much, prices would be expected to drop in accordance with the new nominally reduced amount of money in circulation and things could otherwise carry on as normal. In this instance, however, the North Korean government placed a restriction on the amount of money which could be exchanged: 500,000 won. Given exchange rates at the time, this was the equivalent of approximately US$200. After the week was over the old won was no longer considered legal tender. Anyone who had much more than 500,000 won before the exchange had their personal savings decimated. The currency adjustment was intended to reduce free market activities and to punish those who had been able to generate additional wealth (and with it, additional power) beyond the reach of the North Korean government.[38] [39] [40]

The actions of Francisco Nguema and the North Korean government are examples of the abuse of physical, political and economic power. In many ways they may actually seem counterintuitive. Oppressing an entire nation of people and greatly restricting an individual's economic freedom reduces not only what the oppressed can achieve for themselves and their families but it also massively reduces the contribution they can make overall.

In 1960 "Korea" was among the poorest nations on earth.[41] The south of the country was at least as poor if not poorer than the north. The north had a bigger industrial base to begin with, a larger natural resource allocation and it received substantial aid and industrialisation support from communist supporters; the USSR, China and East Germany. The south subsequently received significant aid, technology transfers and other benefits from the West, but in 1960 the north was by no means starting from behind.[42] Under Kim Il Sung the north adopted the model of Soviet socialism, leading to the abolition of private property and a state-controlled economy. Aside from controlled interaction and trade with other communist nations, interaction with the outside world was (and still is) severely inhibited.[43] The south, under General Park Chung-hee, protected private property rights from 1961 and allowed the private sector to make its own decisions. The government had significant involvement in the economy and agencies including the Economic Planning Board, and the Ministry of Trade and Industry and the Ministry of Finance were established. The focus of these agencies was to support, foster and co-operate with private enterprise as opposed to directing or suppressing it. In addition to receiving some specific technological support from the West, South Koreans were actively encouraged to trade and interact with and leverage the knowledge and economic capacity of the outside world. Economic agencies helped the private sector to produce what the rest of the world wanted.[44]

General Park was not a benevolent guardian, there solely to guide his people to prosperity. He initially came to power via a military coup and under pressure from the US, elections were held in which he was twice democratically returned to power. When he later tried to take permanent control of government and to undo many of the freedoms his government had initially protected, he was eventually assassinated by the head of his own security forces (following several earlier attempts).[45] Like Trotsky before him and Jobs after him, the institutions he had helped to establish were no longer under his control. The institutions he had helped to establish also provided the people of South Korea with a large degree of economic freedom and support under which their economy flourished.

Seventy years of division have seen the south grow to

become the world's twelfth largest economy with a GDP of US$1.8 trillion.[46 47] It has an open, dynamic economy ranked the 19th on the Heritage economic freedom index, with a score of 74.6 placing it above the US, Japan and 157 other nations. The centrally planned, closed and oppressive North is ranked last on the index. It has a score of 3, behind Venezuela with a score of 24.8.[48] North Korea's GDP is estimated at approximately US$40 billion. This equates to about US$1,500 per person. It can be compared against South Korea, which has an output of approximately US$35,000 per person.[47 49] South Koreans can also expect to be between 3 and 8 centimetres taller and to live approximately ten years longer than their northern cousins.[50 51]

North Korea's institutions have protected and provided for three successive generations of the Kim dynasty, but they have aggressively and intentionally suppressed the rights of the North Korean people in order to do so. It may make sense to assume that if the North Korean government had not sought to scuttle private enterprise at every opportunity, that everybody, including the Kims, would be better off. An oppressor can extract more from a US$1.8 trillion economy than from a US$40 billion economy. If Frances Nguema had not destroyed the fishing boats, had not mined the only road in and out of the country or oppressed his most educated citizens his nephew might be worth US$6 billion instead of US$600 million today. But the reality is that the South Korean economy has only grown to the extent that it has because individuals have been able to enjoy the benefit of their increased output and productivity. That is the reason they have sought out better, smarter, more efficient ways of doing things. The North Korean and Equatorial Guinean economy could only grow at anything like the rate enjoyed by South Korea if its people were permitted a greater share of their own increased output. Increased distribution of wealth would mean increased distribution of power, however, diminishing the absolute power enjoyed by its oppressors. For the Kim's, for Frances and Obiang Nguema, the equation is quite simple; increased freedom may increase economic activity, but it would make it harder for them to control and steal from their own people. Better to have absolute power over a small, stifled economy than no control over a growing and prosperous one.

This power is appealing. It can provide security, wealth and luxury beyond anything that might otherwise be possible under a repressive institutional regime. But Francisco Nguema, General Park and many family members and close associates of the Kim dynasty can also attest to the fact that holding on to power is not just a matter of economics. Power held with violence is often taken away with violence, giving oppressors a big reason to hold onto it as tightly as they can.

Equatorial Guineans and North Koreans are born with similar fears, wants, desires and capabilities as the rest of humanity. They are, however, also born into a system of institutions which actively works against their efforts to improve their own lives.

Legitimate violence

Max Weber defines the state as an organisation that has a monopoly on the legitimate use of force within a given area.[52] In the two examples outlined above such a monopoly is being used to oppress citizens of the state. And yet it is often the very absence of such a monopoly under which the greatest tragedies occur. The Siad Barre regime ruled Somalia with a violence and oppression to match that of Francis Nguema.[53] However, it was its collapse in 1991 that caused Somali society to degenerate further into lawlessness, clan conflict, genocide, ongoing civil war and what the United Nations has referred to as the "world's worst humanitarian disaster."[54] [55] Since 1945 an estimated 25 million people have died in civil wars in which there was no clear monopoly on the use of force.[57]

Successive leaders in Equatorial Guinea and North Korea have maintained an iron grip on power, delivering a variation of stability. At the same time, their controls do not allow and do not want individuals to have the freedom to pursue better solutions to their own problems, to gradually improve their own lives over time. In Somalia, an individual's choices are in no way controlled or inhibited by a central government, but they have to fight, not to improve their lives but simply to survive from one day to the next.

When institutions work for us, we can achieve the impossible. Without them our expectations for the future are as certain as whoever wins the next big man showdown. We could not invest in improving our lives or our futures for fear that our output would be taken from us and possibly even used against us. We need institutions, if only to protect us from the coordinated strength of someone else's institution. Like Asimov's robots, our institutions are created by us and were originally intended to serve their creators. Yet when we invest them with the power that they need to perform their function, there is a risk of them evolving and acting in ways we may not have foreseen or intended, particularly under the influence of those who would redirect them to their own benefit.

CHAPTER FIVE

CHAOS AND CONTROL

The fourth line of the Jedi mantra is, "There is no chaos, there is harmony." The Jedi are taught that beneath the apparent chaos in the surrounding universe there is an underlying harmony, that everything has its place and things are playing out just as they should. The Jedi are not passive bystanders, however, as they too have their own role to play. They are trained to be masterful warriors, to manipulate the Force and with it, everything around them. They use their power to fight against evil, to maintain the balance between light and dark. They are guided by a code that requires them to seek peaceful solutions to conflict, to fight only in self-defence and to protect those who are unable to protect themselves. To help them to act in accordance with their code they are also trained to control their emotions, to ensure that their actions are centred in reason, love and compassion, rather than fuelled by fear

and anger. The first and third lines of the Jedi mantra are, "There is no emotion, there is peace - There is no passion, there is serenity." Anakin Skywalker wasn't so good at this bit. He was born and raised a slave until 9 years of age, at which point he was torn away from his mother. The man who pledged to care for him was cut in half shortly thereafter and Anakin was raised by unaffectionate Jedi who helped him to become one of their most powerful members while openly questioning whether he possessed the emotional restraint to wield the power appropriately. Under constant doubt and questioning he was manipulated by an older mentor who validated his pride while inflaming his fears and anger. When finally reunited with his mother, he found that she was being held captive only moments before she died painfully in his arms. He then lost the love of his life in childbirth, believing that his newborn baby(ies) had died with her. All in all, his life was pretty messed up and he understandably struggled to contain his emotions. He loved passionately, he hated, he feared loss and he lashed out in anger and pain. He could not accept that despite his immense power, many things in the universe were outside of his control. Through his fear and anger, he could not see the underlying harmony but only the pain and devastation that a chaotic, disordered universe had in store for him. He was determined to bring a form of order to the galaxy, no matter the cost. Promised a level of power beyond what he could hope to attain as a Jedi – power over others, over life and even over death – Anakin turned to the dark side.[1]
[2]

Darth Marx

Karl Marx's upbringing doesn't appear to have been as traumatic as Anakin Skywalker's, but he still seems to have been equally obsessed with bringing order to a chaotic world. The majority of Marx's economic theories were formed while living in London from the mid-nineteenth century. London at this time was undoubtedly chaotic. It was already the largest city in the world and it was not coping well with a population boom driven by urbanisation and industrialisation. Workers were squeezed into cramped, unsanitary living conditions that lacked the necessary services and infrastructure. They were working an average of 68 hours per week and earning barely enough to feed themselves and their families.[3] An inadequate sewage system saw the Thames clogged with human waste (resulting in a stench so bad that Parliament nearly shifted to Oxford), while burgeoning industry was turning trees, buildings and worker's lungs black with smog and soot.[4] [5] Marx blamed these issues on the capitalist middle class. He saw them as abusing their economic and political power to profit at the expense of the overworked and underpaid working class. Marx's position was based on the belief that those who do the work own the output. He considered the tools, equipment and machinery or "capital" that workers used to be a beneficial feature of the landscape over which no-one could claim ownership, like sun shining on a field. His argument was effectively that these things are an accumulation of worker's efforts at some time in the past, therefore they too belong to the workers. Marx held that these "means of production" had been misappropriated by the capitalist middle class who were then wasting resources in needless competition with each other, trying to maximise profit at the expense of the welfare of the working class. From his perspective the lower classes were being cheated out of their share of output. He believed that the problems he observed could be corrected by overthrowing the seemingly chaotic capitalist system, returning the means of production to the working class and reducing wastage, disorder and inequality through a centrally controlled economy.[6 7 8]

To have any hope of controlling an economy means controlling the institutions of government. In November 1917, Vladimir Lenin led the Bolshevik party in overthrowing the Provisional Government and took control of the Russian parliament and the institutional framework (it was provisional as it had only been in power since March that year following an earlier revolution).[9 10] Lenin was a strong believer in the philosophies of Karl Marx, and once he had gained control of the country's institutions, he set about transforming them to reflect those philosophies. He nationalised industry so that the new government could ensure that the means of production were being utilised to the benefit of the working class (to whom they rightfully belonged), doing away with unnecessary and wasteful competition in the process. Food shortages forced Lenin to initially rely on a compromised form of "state capitalism" where individuals were allowed to own and operate small private enterprises to maintain the agricultural sector while the government continued to control heavy industry, banks and foreign trade. Under pressure from purists following Lenin's death in 1924 and looking to further increase food supply to support the industrialisation effort, Joseph Stalin brought the agricultural sector back under government control.[11]

Stalin's objective was for the Soviet Union to catch up and eventually surpass western economic levels and living standards to prove the superiority of the communist ideology. It was also to protect the Soviets from potential military threats and ultimately to lead a global communist revolution.[12] [13] [14] [15] [16] From 1929 the Soviet industrialisation proceeded faster than that of perhaps any nation before or since. At the beginning of this period approximately 92% of Soviet workers were working in the agricultural sector. Policy focused on converting the economy from a predominantly agricultural to an industrial focus. While this would normally take decades or longer, through the gradual increase of investment of excess production in capital equipment and the redistribution and urbanisation of the workforce from farms to growing factories, the absolute controls assumed by the communist party enabled industrialisation to proceed at a much-accelerated pace. Within two decades the Soviet Union had become the world's largest producer of oil, coal, iron ore and cement.[18] [19] [20] [21] By 1970 just 25% of workers remained focused on agriculture and forestry and it had grown to become the world's second largest economy, by some estimates almost 60% the size of the US. By many measures the living standards of Soviet citizens also improved. Officially there was zero unemployment, and education and literacy levels had improved dramatically.[21] [22] Childhood mortality dropped, along with the incidence of a range of diseases and by the late 1950s life expectancy for the average Soviet citizen had risen by over 25 years.[23] [24] The Soviets were held up by many as a model for other industrialising nations to follow. Even developed nations took note. The Communist Party USA reached a peak membership of 200,000, and in 1945 the Communist Party of Canada received over 2% of the popular vote and won a seat in parliament.[25] [26] In 1949 the Japanese Communist Party won 10% of the national vote.[27] Where they didn't have electoral success communist parties and ideologies had an influence over a broad range of areas, most notably the labour movement and the growth of unionism. Developed nations also nationalised many key industries, taking over from the private sector in the provision of a number of goods and services. The UK, for example, nationalised a broad range of industries including the liquor trade, media (the BBC was a privately owned company until 1927), transport services (including British Airways, also privately owned until 1939), as well as coal, petrol, steel and gas industries and numerous utilities.[28] [29] [30] [31] By the late 1970s nationalised industry made up approximately 10% of Britain's GDP.[32] France's post-war economy was categorised by the term "dirigisme", from the French diriger or "to direct", referring to the influence of the government in directing economic activity.[33] In Japan the Ministry of International Trade and Industry was deeply involved in directing the economy.[34]

Limits of control

While Japanese and Western government institutions engaged directly with their economies, there was a limit to the controls they put in place. Communist parties never really got close to governing in these nations, while the post-World War Two US Marshall recovery plan also tied aid payments to economic modernisation, productivity improvements and maintenance of free and competitive markets.[35 36] The Soviets and their allies were offered aid under the plan but refused on the grounds that it would require them to open up their economies. But the Soviet model had begun to show its vulnerabilities long before the end of the second world war.

While industrialisation would eventually benefit the sector, between 1932 and 1934 the forced collectivisation and premature shift of resources away from agriculture contributed to a famine that resulted in between 5 to 8 million deaths.[37 38 39] Rationing and shortages of consumer goods became commonplace, first as planners focused efforts on production of industrial goods and later as a result of the misallocation of resources and inefficiencies resulting in the underproduction of most consumer goods. Stalin was also forced to make his own compromises to the communist ideal, permitting higher rates of pay for managers and specialists against further opposition from within the party.[40] Details of wage rates were rarely made public but while this was perceived by the outside world as an attempt to hide the reality of low wages in comparison to developed nations, it also appears to have been about hiding significant disparity across roles and sectors internally. Wages could be spent in nominated stores where a person's occupation or party connections could provide access to special privileges and special prices. Such occupations were themselves up for sale. Management positions could often be secured by bribing party officials. The higher the position and the better the privileges, the bigger the bribe. Factory managers trying to meet quotas but restricted by a government set wage schedule would try to offer other incentives to attract the better workers. The first trick was to never to produce too much in the first place, keeping expected output low and increasing the likelihood of meeting subsequent targets and maximising their own and employees' output linked bonuses. To hit targets managers would often falsify results, let quality slip, or both. Complying with wage and other directives (or at least appearing to comply) led to many costly administrative overheads.[41] In one calculation, historian Donald Fitzer found that the determination of a machinist's monthly wage and bonus required approximately 8 kilograms of paper and 8,500 signatures at a cost equal to 22% of the worker's annual wage.[42] Such overheads likely helped to maintain the Soviets' claim to zero unemployment with everyone gainfully, if not productively, employed.

Manipulation of the wage and bonus systems generally wasn't enough to provide workers with a decent standard of living. Managers would turn a blind eye to an employee's theft of goods, which would be traded on the black market in exchange for other misappropriated or privately produced goods. By the 1970s an estimated 30% of household income was coming from illegal economic activity, and approximately 10 to 12% of the labour force was believed to be employed in the "second economy". These activities thrived despite a minimum five-year prison term for speculative trading. Black markets were not just distributing the stolen wares of the government-controlled producers, however, and wherever possible they also sought to fill the gaps in official production through private producers and service providers. Activities in this sector were generally overlooked because almost everyone was in on it. It's estimated that less than 1% of crimes of speculation were reported to authorities and it's widely believed that without the second economy the Soviet system would not have survived as long as it did.[43] [44]

People generally weren't going to prison for trading on the black market but they were for other reasons. Forced labour camps or "Gulags" saw up to 14 million prisoners between 1929 and 1953. Many of these were political prisoners or petty criminals, often convicted without trial.[45] [46] [47] Simply making a joke about the Soviet government could result in imprisonment – there was even a joke about that; A judge walks out of his chambers laughing his head off. A colleague approaches him and asks why he is laughing. "I just heard the funniest joke in the world!" "Well, go ahead, tell me!" says the other judge. "I can't – I just gave someone ten years for it!"[48 49] But life in the labour camps was no joke. Prisoners were forced to perform hard physical labour in very poor conditions that resulted in approximately 1.7 million deaths between 1929 and 1953.[50] Outside of deaths in the prison system, Stalin instigated the execution of approximately one million people between 1936 and 1938. Known retrospectively as "the Great Purge", the executions were intended to solidify Stalin's grip on power and ultimately impacted people from all walks of life, including party and military officials.[51 52]

For some, for Stalin, Lenin and Marx perhaps, the inequalities, shortages, famines, corruption, imprisonments and executions may have been acceptable sacrifices on the road to achieving the communist dream of a classless society. But to lead the global communist revolution the Soviets needed to prove the superiority of their system in providing for the needs of its people, and by the 1970s economic growth had begun to slow. In 1950 the Soviet Union had GDP of US$2841 per capita, compared against Austria, which had US$3706. By 1973 the Soviet GDP had more than doubled to US$6059. Although the Austrian GDP had tripled in the same time frame, Soviet growth was still respectable. By 1990, however, Austrian output had continued to grow, now to over four times the 1950s level, and Soviet growth had stalled. Other eastern bloc nations fared even worse. In 1938 Austria had an equivalent output to Czechoslovakia, but by 1990 they were producing nearly six times as much.[53] The Soviets had first benefited from gains that could be achieved by clever, yet relatively straightforward adjustments to the economy; from increasing the capital stock, importing advanced technologies, improving education levels and industrialisation. Moreso than other communist nations they also then benefited from rising prices for coal, oil and gas. When energy prices crashed in 1973, the underlying weaknesses of the Soviet economy could no longer be hidden. The early gains from industrialisation and modernisation were being offset by inefficiencies, corruption and a lack of innovation.[53] [54] [55] [56]

From Eastern to Western Europe, North to South Korea, China to Japan, even in the microcosms of individual cities such as Berlin or Kolkata, real world experimentation continuously revealed the limitations and pitfalls of absolute control. The economy was too complex for planners to understand and effectively direct. The lack of opportunity for personal gain within the formal system took away any reason workers or prospective entrepreneurs might have had to perform their allocated tasks particularly well, or to come up with new and better ways of doing things. If there was an opportunity for personal gain it was more likely to be found either in the black markets or in gaming the controlled economy. Governments could not replicate or make up for the innate human drivers, or the incentives, efficiencies and innovations that they contributed to and which drove other economies. They had no way of duplicating the processing power of the millions of minds, leveraging their own very specific understanding of their own problems, objectives, strengths and weaknesses, to engage in many millions of transactions every day in domestic, foreign or even their own black markets. The planners could not accurately determine who needed how much of what to allocate resources and production effort appropriately. This not only resulted in shortages of consumer goods, but also industrial inputs. Even where the necessary materials were available, managers and workers were incentivised to produce just enough to maximise their bonuses but not too much that their quotas would be increased. With no private ownership or unemployment there were few positive or negative incentives. There were no owners risking their savings on a factory's profitability and all that encompasses.

The means of production are not like sun shining on a field. Even when they were built by workers at some time in the past, someone likely had to design them, organise their construction, provide the materials, pay the workers and arrange for their maintenance. These are all separate activities involving risk, resources and effort that are unlikely to be undertaken without the expectation of sufficient reward. Managers and workers generally did the minimum amount of work required of them. They faced little risk of losing their jobs – the system basically guaranteed them another. Everyone was incentivised to steal whatever they could get away with. The lack of competition meant that there was no inbuilt process for retaining good decisions, designs, processes, employees or managers, or deselecting bad ones. With few alternatives for most goods and services, end consumer's levels of satisfaction or dissatisfaction had little impact on what was produced. It was not the consumer's but the planner's decision how much of what should be produced and who should produce it. And if anyone complained too loudly, they had a good chance of being shipped off to a labour camp they might never come back from.

In 1985 Mikhail Gorbachev moved to reform the Soviet economy under the banner of "perestroika", or restructuring. He was the first Soviet leader in its 63-year history to publicly admit that things weren't working and that they needed to try something new. Not much changed at first but a law introduced in 1988 permitted the private ownership of manufacturing, services and import-export businesses. Three years later the Soviet Union and the Soviet economic experiment were over.[57] [58]

An economy that is free to move in accordance with the desires and considerations of its participants can appear chaotic. There will be businesses that thrive as some fail, and others who take their place. Products will be invented, refined and discontinued. Every day, hundreds if not thousands of people will lose their jobs, while thousands more begin something new. All the while governments, media and special interest groups of all sorts will be trying to push things one way or another. It can appear to be a disordered, volatile and frantic free-for-all. Where no individual or group is telling every other individual or group what to do and how to do it, each participant, with personalities as distinctive as fingerprints, will make their own slightly idiosyncratic decisions and follow their own strategies for achieving their objectives. People will make mistakes, waste time, energy and resources, lose their jobs and their businesses, they'll vote for inept politicians and enact foolish legislation and they will struggle, sometimes just to stay alive.

The Soviets saw these flaws as a consequence of an unrestrained, free market economy, and believed they could do a better job. They thought the economy could be accurately perceived and controlled from what Lenin referred to as the "commanding heights."[59] They viewed competition as an unnecessary side-effect of capitalist greed that led to wasted resources which could be eliminated by entrusting a benevolent central body with the responsibility for directing all economic activity. They also thought that individuals would be willing to work hard and to find ways to increase output for the collective good regardless of how much, when or if they would ever personally benefit from their efforts. The solution outlined by Marx and implemented by Lenin and Stalin did bring a form of order which did lead to some improvements for some people in the short term, but it also took away people's capacity to influence their own quality of life, disabling the primary force that drives an economy forward. The Soviets viewed the economy like someone who saw the Great Barrier Reef from space and claimed it was one big, long rock, and failed to appreciate the delicate harmony of the many millions of motivated, self-directed organisms that make up the whole.

Everyone wants a piece

At the extremes a government can completely control and oppress its people or leave them exposed to chaos and lawlessness. Soviet controls were clearly excessive, but what exactly constitutes the controls likely to stifle an economy's core drivers is difficult to determine – and yet, controls of some sort are inevitable. Government influences the economy through its very existence. Beyond its role as consumer and service provider, non-economic controls such as those put in place to protect the rights of citizens or to maintain a border can have significant economic consequences, both positive and negative. A government who wanted to completely avoid exerting any influence on an economy would soon see that government is not the only institution capable of restricting economic freedom.

Religions have been doing it probably for as long as any form of government. The Rigveda, a foundational Hindu text from approximately 1500 BCE, tells the story of

Purusha, a cosmic being from which all creation emerges. The four Varnas or classes of people emerge from Purusha's body. The Brahmins, priests and the scholarly class emerged from Purusha's mouth, the Kshatriyas or ruling and military class from its arms, the Vaishyas, including farmers, traders and artisans from its thighs while the Shudras, manual labourers and servants emerged from its feet. The story of Purusha provides the spiritual foundation for the Hindu caste system, within which an individual's caste or jāti is hereditarily defined, severely limiting social and economic mobility. Most religious texts contain references outlining how certain tasks should be performed and who should perform them.[60][61] Of the 6,226 verses in the Quran there are over 1,400 verses addressing economic issues.[62] Many of these and similar guidance at the heart of other religions have undoubtedly contributed to social and economic cohesion in groups adhering to their teachings and many are very similar to modern non-secular laws that cover a wide variety of business and economic practices such as fair dealing and anti-competitive practices. As a result, even when it is not their stated intent, many also seriously impact economic freedoms.[63]

Businesses will also push for whatever privileges or restrictions that might help to make their enterprise more profitable, seeking to influence governments to enact laws to suit their needs.[64] There's an estimated 100,000 lobbyists in the US paid to influence government policies.[65] In the run up to the 2016 federal election, the

US financial sector spent about US$2 billion trying to influence the outcome of the election.[66] One of lobbyists more impressive achievements was to have pizza recognised as a vegetable.[67]

In an effort to improve the nutritional value of school lunches, the US Department of Agriculture (USDA) wanted to update its nutritional guidelines, reducing the number of potatoes and increasing the number of green vegetables served. They also wanted to remove an existing provision which assessed two tablespoons of tomato paste as of equivalent nutritional value to half a cup of vegetables. While this seemed a reasonable proposal from a nutritional standpoint it was a big problem for some food manufacturers. In particular, the frozen pizza industry had, up until that point, relied on the provision to help maintain annual government subsidised sales of approximately US$500 million worth of frozen pizza into the public school system. The change would mean that a slice of pizza would need to come with a half a cup of tomato sauce or, according to a letter to the USDA from the National Frozen Pizza Institute (an actual organisation), so much that a slice of pizza would be swimming in tomato sauce, making it "incapable of holding cheese and other toppings." After intense lobbying from "the Institute" and other impacted organisations, Congress blocked the proposed changes. Pizza lobbyists probably had a point, as there are in fact quite a lot of nutrients in tomato paste. But it also tends to be packed with salt, it's generally not as good for you as half a cup of fresh vegetables and it's definitely not as filling, which is why you wouldn't expect your kids to be satisfied with a few tablespoons of tomato paste for dinner and the reason it needs to be supplemented by a bunch of other less healthy stuff to be called a meal.[67] [68] [69]

By its nature, lobbying is intended to promote the needs of special interest groups. If your needs are aligned with this group, you might be happy with the changes they bring about. Alongside the members of the National Frozen Pizza Institute there are probably millions of pizza-loving school children who are very happy that their pizza still has room for pepperoni. But changes intended to benefit one group don't necessarily benefit society as a whole, and sometimes they do real damage. A 2009 IMF report found that banks' lobbying efforts in the US between 2000 and 2006 helped drive a deterioration in lending standards which then contributed to the 2007 housing crash and the subsequent financial crisis.[70]

Sometimes when businesses can't convince governments to change or uphold laws in their favour, they'll just go and make up their own. Thomas Edison may not have invented the very first electric light bulb but in 1879 he did produce the first version that could be practically useful; an oxygen-free bulb with a carbon filament that could burn for over 40 hours.[71] Before long everyone wanted electric lighting and thousands of manufacturers were lining up to sell it to them (from backyard workshops to companies that remain household names today).

Manufacturers were desperate for any advantage and the technology evolved quickly. By the mid-1920s, a household light bulb could burn for 2,500 hours or more. It was great for consumers who benefited from improving quality, competitive prices and longer lasting bulbs, but it wasn't easy for manufacturers to keep up with constantly evolving technology and intense competition.[72] After a particularly tumultuous period in which they saw their sales drop by half, German manufacturer, Osram, decided something needed to change. On 23rd December, 1924, Osram chairman, Wilhelm Meinhardt, together with representatives from General Electric, Philips, Tungsram and other bulb manufacturers, established the "Convention for the Development and Progress of the Incandescent Electric Lamp Industry", to become known as "the Phoebus Cartel". In a manner not that uncommon at the time, the cartel sought to control the sale and manufacture of light bulbs by setting production quotas and levying significant fines for overproduction. They also came up with an ingenious way of improving the profitability of their respective businesses – they would reduce their light bulbs' average burning time, forcing their customers to buy more of them. Applying the same level of engineering brilliance and enthusiasm for making a profit that had helped them to increase the bulb's lifespan 60-fold in just over 40 years, cartel members methodically set about refining their products to ensure that they would burn for 1,000 hours and no more. They were serious about it, too. Hundreds of factories covered under the agreement would send samples to a Swiss laboratory responsible for testing their performance, and if a bulb burnt longer or shorter than it was supposed to, the factory would be fined. The directive had its desired effect, and between 1926 and 1934 the average lifespan of bulbs produced by factories regulated by the cartel reduced from 1800 to 1205 hours. Japanese producer, Tokyo Electric, even complained that the reduced lifespan had contributed to a fivefold increase in sales which was making it very difficult for them to hold production within their allotted quota. It was difficult for member firms to act against the directives, however, most were either wholly or partially owned by General Electric or were licensed by them to produce their patented bulbs, further strengthening the cartel's influence.[73 74]

The cartel remained in place for 15 years before World War Two ended cooperation between the member companies. By that stage smaller, non-member producers were also having an impact on the market with their own bulbs, which would burn for much longer than 1,000 hours. The cartel eventually disbanded but the damage had been done. While they had continued to make improvements in some areas, the focus on a shorter lifespan plus the opportunity cost of having many of their brightest minds focused on delivering a deliberately underperforming product likely set the industry back decades. They also invented a concept that continues to cause us to wonder whether a manufacturer intended for their product to suspiciously fall apart or breakdown shortly after its warranty expiration – "planned obsolescence".

The cartel is not just a tool for big business. Before there were even corporations to form cartels, markets throughout Europe were dominated by members of various professions who banded together in guilds. From the early Middle Ages, guilds closely guarded the secrets of their respective crafts, sharing their knowledge only with people they believed could be trusted, through a master and apprentice system and actively, even violently, restricting the activities of non-member practitioners. Through this system guild members were able to restrict the supply of skilled craftsmen, driving up prices for their services and controlling and often restricting technological advances that may have otherwise reduced reliance on their knowledge and experience. Guilds often required apprentices to undergo needlessly long training periods, during which the guild itself and their respective masters would profit from their work. Apprentices would then need to donate money or goods to finally be granted membership.[75] Guilds did play a role in maintaining quality and transferring knowledge and skills in their respective professions (Universities of Oxford, Cambridge, Paris and Bologna were all founded on centralised communities of guilds), but in most cases it was the eventual widespread decline of guilds that provided real economic benefit, leading to an end to the secrecy, a wider sharing of knowledge and skills and a lowering of prices for their previously monopolised services.[76]

Guilds did not disappear completely. Even today many professional groups maintain organisations with a significant impact (if not complete control) on the training and licensing of new entrants into their own field. The American Medical Association represents the interests of US doctors and medical students. They have long fought against allowing nurse practitioners and other health professionals from performing tasks otherwise restricted to their own members, even in the face of a dangerous shortage of qualified doctors.[77] [78] At the same time, Labour unions bring together affiliated professionals to protect their interests, but those interests do not always align with those of the broader society. A powerful labour union or professional association can manipulate the supply of labour, pushing for higher wages or improved conditions for their members, sometimes at the cost of reducing an industry or an economy's competitiveness – which leads to higher costs for consumers and reduced employment opportunities for outsiders. It may even be against their interests to increase productivity. If a union charges a fixed fee per member, then they may be motivated to maximise the number of workers in the industry (and in their union), rather than supporting the industry to maintain or improve efficiencies of the existing labour force. Public sector unions involved in the provision of monopoly services such as public transport or postal services tend to be in a very strong position when it comes to getting what they want, with strikes leaving consumers with little alternative and causing significant disruption. A 2015 strike on the London tube has been estimated to have cost the economy as much as GBP300 million in just 24 hours.[79] Whether this action was justified or not, unions, like other powerful groups, can abuse their position and they can also be manipulated for individual gain. There are countless examples of union agendas being hijacked by individuals or other, often criminal groups. The history of trade unions is often intertwined with that of organised crime. In an investigation into the Painters and Dockers Union in Australia in 1980, the head of the investigation, Frank Costigan, noted that, "Violence is the means by which they control the members of their group. They do not hesitate to kill."[80] More recently in 2014, an investigation into corruption in the construction sector in Quebec, Canada, revealed an abuse of power among Union officials along with deep and continuing ties to organised crime.[81]

Religions, corporations, professional associations, labour unions and other groups may have strong and even moral arguments for the privileges and restrictions they want in place, but more often than not their actions benefit one group while limiting the freedom of another. There is a well held belief that the story of the Varnas emerging from Purusha's various body parts was not written along with the original Rigveda text but was inserted sometime later as a charter myth, written to justify the prevailing social hierarchy, further entrenching the privilege enjoyed by the upper classes and restricting the economic and social mobility of the lower classes.[82] Even the concepts of karma and reincarnation, central to Hindu philosophy, arguably provide spiritual justification for the caste system, underlying the importance of accepting your preordained fate and performing your role without complaint in the hope of being reborn on a higher plane in the next life. We don't know when the verse introducing this class division was written, and we don't know who wrote it, but it probably wasn't a member of the Shudra class.

The Phoebus Cartel also presented itself as existing to serve a higher purpose. The original convention signed by its founding members spoke of quality and uniformity in the industry and of increasing the use and effectiveness of electric lighting all to the "advantage of the consumer." But that was a front put forward to hide its variably illegal and invariably immoral actions. It purposefully limited competition and progress in a burgeoning industry, binding and restricting the freedoms of potential competitors while committing them to a substandard product designed to extract undue profits from a deceived and manipulated marketplace.

We might be part of, or have sympathy for, a labour union or a professional association. They might also rightly be fighting for smaller incremental and necessary gains, or against a restriction or privilege granted to a corporation or assumed by a government. They are often fighting for diffused interests which in aggregate can make a big difference to the individual but for which, in isolation, few individuals would have the resources to stand up and fight for. In 1888, women's rights activist, Annie Besant, wrote an article describing the horrible conditions being endured by workers at the Bryant and May match factory in Bow, London. The women and teenage girls employed at the factory worked 14-hour days under constant exposure to white phosphorous, which was cheaper than the safer red phosphorous but could cause a horrific form of bone cancer. They were subject to a system of fines for various offences, which would further reduce their already meagre salaries. Workers could be fined for dropping matches, talking or going to the toilet without permission, and running late for work would cost them half a day's pay. In an effort to dispute the article, factory management tried to force their employees to sign a contradictory statement, leading to the sacking of one employee who refused to sign. In response, approximately 1,400 staff walked out in protest. Their complaints and their actions received a groundswell of public support and led to several improvements in their situation – including an end to the fines system and the eventual banning of the use of white phosphorus in matches. The success of the Bryant and May match workers strike inspired the growth of unions across the country, which undoubtedly contributed to improvements in the working conditions and benefits of their members. But with sufficient power, unions and professional associations can quickly move beyond protecting the rights of their own members to directly intruding on the rights of others.[83] [84] The California Correctional Peace Officers Association (CCPOA) raises approximately US$23 million per year in membership dues. Despite having only one tenth the membership base they spend more on lobbying and political donations than the California Teachers Association or any other union in California, totalling approximately US$8 million per year. They spend it very effectively, too. California's prison guards earn nearly 60% above the national average, despite California having the highest recidivism rate in the US.[85] In addition to fighting for better pay and conditions for its members, the CCPOA advocates "for the laws, funding and policies needed to improve prison operations and protect public safety."[86] On this basis they have continuously lobbied for laws increasing prison terms and incarceration rates to help create some of the harshest sentencing laws in the country. You might think that the CCPOA would focus its efforts on improving conditions and wages for its members, leaving decisions on sentencing laws and prison terms to the courts and legislators, but as criminologist and Stanford Law Professor, Joan Petersilia, puts it, "more prisoners lead to more prisons; more prisons require more guards; more guards means more dues-paying members and fund-raising capability; and fundraising, of course, translates into political influence." Keeping prisons full is just too important to the CCPOA. Their success means restricting not just the economic, but also the physical freedom of others.[87]

An economy rewards people for coming up with new and improved solutions to our problems, which in turn encourages competition and diversity, further improving the available solutions over time. Left alone however, an economy is not very good at solving the problem of people directing accumulated rewards and power toward reducing competition and diversity to their own advantage. The free market greatly rewarded Thomas Edison and General Electric for providing affordable electric lighting to the world. These rewards have motivated General Electric, its investors and its employees to continue innovating and helping us solve many of our problems for over 125 years. But in 1925, when faced with falling profits and declining market share, they were not averse to using their position to suppress competition and innovation to the detriment of the consumer and society as a whole.

Each of the above groups and the individuals they represent have a right to fight for their own self-interest. Labour unions fight for the rights and conditions of workers, corporations represent the interest of shareholders, democratically elected governments exist for the benefit of the people they represent. As each group pushes for controls that benefit its own members – or members of a subgroup – they invariably infringe on the freedoms of others. If not, there probably wouldn't have been much to fight about in the first place. But when we as a society value the right of the individual to work unrestrained toward the maintenance and improvement of their own existence, then we deny the right of others, of individuals, corporations, trade unions, religions, lobby groups and of governments, to unjustly or unnecessarily restrict those efforts. This is a trade-off that can only be maintained with effort and all manner of finely balanced controls.

Controlled chaos

In 483 AD the constitution of Byzantine emperor Zeno allowed for the punishment of monopolistic behaviour and voided any existing monopoly rights, even those previously granted by the state.[88] 1,100 years later the English courts referenced Zeno's constitution in the case of Darcy vs Allein, after Queen Elizabeth granted a member of her court exclusive rights to manufacture playing cards. The court stated that monopolies are not conducive "to the benefit of the common weal but to its ruin and damage." They declared that the enforcement of monopoly rights is solely to the benefit of the monopolist, that it restricts potential competitors from accessing the market and that it is likely to result in higher prices without any incentives to maintain or improve quality. Politely they also suggested that the Queen must have been deceived and that enforcing the patent would promote "idleness" among non-patented playing card manufacturers.[89]

In the US in 1890 the Sherman Antitrust Act sought to prohibit anti-competitive behaviour, such as restriction of supply, price fixing or monopolistic behaviour, and was successfully used to break up John D. Rockefeller's

Standard Oil.[90] [91] It was specifically directed at US trusts which were being used to coordinate control of multiple businesses for the purpose of forming virtual monopolies, but it did not quite have the fully desired effect. Businesses realised the Act could be circumvented by simply merging with their former trust partners, setting off the biggest wave of corporate mergers in US history. The Clayton Act introduced in 1914 subsequently tried to plug this gap by restricting mergers which would substantially reduce competition and restricting anyone from being a director of two or more competing businesses.[92] Throughout the twentieth century an ever-increasing number of nations saw similar measures introduced.

While it was intended to rein in the anti-competitive practices of big business, the Sherman Act was also used against labour unions whose strikes and boycotts were judged as a form of restraint of trade, forbidden under the Act. Unions and guilds and their negotiation techniques have drifted between legal and illegal for hundreds of years and their standing and rights in many nations was still not totally clear. Modern labour laws represent a fine balance of the rights and limitations placed both on employers, employees and employee unions from restricting each other's economic freedoms and maintaining unrestricted access to both business and employment opportunities. The full title of the 1935 US National Labour Relations Act is, "An act to diminish the causes of labour disputes burdening or obstructing interstate and foreign commerce, to create a National

Labor Relations Board, and for other purposes." The Act recognises the advantage that large corporations or industry groups might have over single employees, allowing workers a mechanism for forming institutions capable of collective actions such as strikes or negotiations, counterbalancing the power and influence of corporations. Through its wording it also puts limits on the power of unions themselves, protecting an individual's right not to join a union.[93 94] Together with the 1947 Taft-Hartley Act it further limits the union's capacity to discriminate against non-union backed employees, employers, suppliers or customers.[95]

These laws – and many more like them – exist to limit the capacity of powerful groups to interfere with a market's functioning and to make the cost and implications of doing so less attractive than focusing their resources on those activities most likely to ensure their continued existence in a dynamic, competitive marketplace; building a better product, delivering a better service, effectively representing the interests of their stakeholders. Of course, these laws have evolved under the guidance of bureaucrats and representatives already under the influence of powerful groups within our imperfect democratic systems.

Apparent chaos

While we generally want to do the right thing, whatever that may be, if the most effective way of achieving our objectives involves abusing the power we hold over others, we'll probably do that, even if that requires us to come up with justifications for our abuses in the process. But if the system within which we exist makes achieving our goals through the abuse of power more difficult than achieving those goals through delivering value to the people around us, then this is where we will expend our efforts.

A cause may be justified, there may be valid reasons for the privileges or restrictions that a group is fighting for. But regardless of their real or stated motivation, controls restricting economic freedom handicap the motivations, processing power and efforts of other contributors. What begins as an entirely free and open economy will be exploited by groups and individuals who, like all of us, are seeking to survive and prosper, and who will likely capitalise on anything that enables them to shift power and privilege to their advantage. Monarchs, elected officials, dictators, doctors, workers, priests and scholars, light bulb and frozen pizza manufacturers would all forgo a little chaos for controls in their favour. If we're really lucky, the groups that gain power might fight for restrictions and privileges that benefit us as individuals in the short term. We might even be one of the elite, our power and privilege compensating us for the slow pace of improvement or decline in quality of life being experienced more broadly. But in the long term, restrictions on a society's freedom and capacity to solve its problems impact everyone. And if we are lucky enough to be represented by a powerful group in the short term, we might have the sense to realise that this group may not always be the most powerful and may not always accurately reflect our desires. We might instead hope therefore, for a form of governance that represents all of us equally and enforces selective controls that restrict freedoms only when absolutely necessary. Because diversity, experimentation and constant change, which give the appearance of chaos, are precisely the things that make an economy dynamic, responsive and capable of continuing to deliver better solutions to our problems over time.

The alternatives

The overcrowded, unsanitary living conditions and poor working conditions of 1850s London were a consequence of huge increases in economic activity, productivity and growth, which provided real benefit to the people of London. However, they also created huge problems for the people living and working there at the time. They were problems for which no group or individual could be blamed or forced to correct and which, as Marx observed, were inherent in the capitalist system, the result of many thousands of workers and businesses each selfishly working to improve their own existence. If the people of London had a Lenin or a Trotsky to inspire them, they might have fought a Soviet style revolution, trashing the system altogether and replacing it with something much more considered, structured and less chaotic. Instead, in

1855, after a particularly hot and smelly summer, the democratically elected British parliament passed the Metropolis Management Act which led to the creation of the Metropolitan Board of Works. Tasked with establishing infrastructure and improving living conditions for London residents, the Board built numerous bridges, roads and parks, and set about solving the city's sewage problem by installing nearly 1800 kilometres of main and street sewers. Residents had many criticisms of the Board, which was overseen by nominees from the vestries rather than directly elected representatives.[96] In 1889 it was replaced by the London City Council. Elected by the people of London, the Council still makes a lot of mistakes and receives plenty of criticism, but with selective controls and a property tax linked to home values, it has so far managed to maintain a largely effluent-free Thames without completely discarding the freedoms and principles which enable modern economies to flourish and thrive.[97]

A certain balance between chaos and control is necessary for a well-functioning economy. Too many controls stifle individual motivation, resourcefulness and experimentation. Too few controls reduce the willingness of individuals to transact beyond close family and social networks, significantly reducing the benefits otherwise available through cooperation, specialisation and trade. A lack of appropriate controls will then likely be exploited by groups and individuals with power to implement their own controls, ones designed to build and cement their own advantages at the expense of the economic freedoms of others.

Like the Jedi, we need to recognise the harmony in the apparent chaos, using our powers sparingly, to defend our own and others' right to self-determination from the various forces that might seek to control us.

CHAPTER SIX

NO SUPERHEROES

There's lots of different types of superheroes with different superpowers. Some are strong, some can fly, some are immortal or simply can't be hurt. For all their differences, a superhero, by nature, is good. If they're not good, then they're the villain, not the hero. A superhero knows the difference between right and wrong and they always choose right. When we're kids this seems like the easy part of being a superhero – but as we get older, we begin to understand just how difficult it is. The world is not comprised of goodies and baddies, it's complex, grey and constantly changing. Superheroes are wish-fulfilment. We wish we had their powers, or we wish they had our backs when we need them, but we also like to think that there's someone out there who knows what's right. Freud would say that the appeal of superheroes, like the appeal of gods, stems from our childhood perception of our parents as all-good, all-knowing and all-powerful, and the desire to feel that level of comfort and reassurance later in life.[1] This desire also plays a role in politics and economics.

In 3000 BCE, Egyptian kings took the role of the gods' representative on earth before becoming an actual god upon their death.[2] Monarchs and emperors throughout history have often claimed a connection to the divine. Even the Kim dynasty, officially an atheist state, uses the appeal of a superhero or God-King to solidify its grip on power. According to North Korea's state-run media, Kim Jong Il could walk at three weeks of age, scored a perfect 300 the first time he bowled and scored five hole-in-ones the first time he played golf. Kim Jong Un could apparently drive from three years of age and was a competitive sailor at nine.[3] Together with North Korean scientists he formulated a drug which cures or treats AIDS, cancer, Ebola, heart disease, the common cold and even aging.[4]

Karl Marx did not believe in the deification of an all-powerful leader and spoke out against personality cults – and even his own fame – but he still believed in a superhero, of sorts. Marxism was dependent on a superhero proletariat, willing to act in the best interest of a collective society, working for the benefit of all and ignoring their own self-interest and the level of their individual reward. They would be led by an equally heroic and incorruptible central planner, working solely in the interest of society and able to do what no human had ever done before; to understand the economy well enough to allocate labour and resources in a manner that would maximise efficiency and output.[5]

Ayn Rand is perhaps the ideological opposite of Karl Marx. She is a champion of individual accountability and hates government intervention. Her utopia was the ultimate meritocracy, where superior individuals were the engines of human society, delivering growth through innovation, risk-taking and purpose-driven individual effort.[6] Rand's protagonists possessed near perfect intellect and were untouchable in their respective fields. They were morally unimpeachable and would never lie, cheat, steal, bribe or collude, as they never had to. They were self-made, super rich, never went broke and never had to struggle or watch their own businesses decline or fail. They were also superheroes.

Rand and Marx had very different views on humanity, the rights of the individual and the preferred role of government. Yet the driving force behind their respective utopias, the reason that both are incompatible with the real world, is that they were based on morally incorruptible persons whose actions, either entirely selfish in Rand's world or entirely selfless in Marx's world, would be the driving force of abundance and prosperity. Rand hated Marx's idolisation of the working class and Marx would have despised Rand's industrialists, as both, correctly, saw them for the fantasies they were.

No superheroes

True democracy is held up as the political end goal of civilised societies. But its strength as a political system does not come from superheroes or even from leveraging the virtues of humanity; it comes from mitigating their weaknesses.

If Rand hated Marx, she really hated C.S. Lewis. She referred to the British author as an "abysmal bastard", a "monstrosity", a "cheap, awful, miserable, touchy, social-meta-physical mediocrity", and a "God-damn, beaten mystic".[7] Lewis was a devout Christian whose famous "Chronicles of Narnia" is a broad retelling of the story of Christ.[8] But whatever his thoughts on God, Lewis was not a believer in everyday superheroes. He did not believe in democracy, as humanity was "so wise and good that everyone deserved a share in the government." In contrast, he stated, "I do not deserve a share in governing a hen-roost much less a nation. Nor do most people … The real reason for democracy is just the reverse. Mankind is so fallen that no man can be trusted with unchecked power over his fellows."[9] Modern democracy is based on the continuous transition of power to ensure that no group or individual can take control of the institution of government and direct it toward their benefit. Democracy does not require humanity to be more or better to function. Instead, it mitigates against the propensity of individuals and groups to prioritise their own needs, to the detriment of others.

The word "democracy" comes from the Greek "demos" (meaning people) and "kratos" (meaning power) – power to the people (right on).[10] The essence of democracy is the decentralisation or distribution of ultimate power over the institution of government, to those being governed. There are a lot of things that work against a true distribution of political power, with the biggest obstacle usually being those who hold the power in the first place. But distribution of power is also not just the end goal of democracy – it is also its foundation.

When a single group or individual holds all the power, like the God-Kings of ancient Egypt or a modern-day dictator, then there is no reason to share or compromise power. With the first fracturing of power comes the first compromise. Two groups or individuals with power either fight to diminish one another's power, as is perhaps more often the case, or they can learn to compromise, content in the knowledge that they at least continue to have more power than everyone else. In thirteenth century England, rebel barons forced King John to accept their demands for reforms (later to become enshrined in the Magna Carta), dramatically altering the balance of power (King John first tried to see off this threat by reaching out to the other regional power of the time, the Catholic church, promising to join the crusades in exchange for their support).[11] Power fractured again during the industrial revolution, with the rise of the economically powerful merchant class which demanded rights and representation equivalent to that enjoyed by the ruling elite.

Nobody likes uncertainty, particularly those who are used to knowing what is going to happen next. If they can't hold on to absolute power, the powerful will settle for rights and protections that they had previously denied others. It is a powerful shift from worrying about controlling others to not allowing others to control them. As more and more people make a claim to self-determination and having a say in the decisions that impact them, it becomes harder and harder to argue that these rights should not apply to others. Opponents arguing against such a system do so at their own risk, as winning the argument does not mean that they necessarily also win the power and benefits. And once power has been fractured and mechanisms for maintaining its distribution are in place, there is a greater resistance to the accumulation and abuse of power by any individual or small group.

All democratic governments have inbuilt mechanisms for the peaceful transition of power. At multiple levels regular elections force the governed to confirm their previous selections or to elect somebody new. Elected officials know that if voters don't like the decisions they make, they will be removed from power. For many elected positions – such as the US and South Korean presidency – no individual can serve more than a predetermined maximum term before they are forced to step down. This limits elected officials' capacity to amend laws that might lead to abuses of power or extend their grip on power.

Fragile

Throughout most of human history, democracy has been relatively rare. Conceptually it is easier to maintain a democratic system in a smaller nation where lifestyles and preferences are aligned. As a society or nation grows, increasingly disparate views increase the likelihood of one group seeing benefit in having greater levels of power. Alternatively, if a society remains small it is at risk of being absorbed or destroyed by a larger, stronger neighbour. Fracturing of power may facilitate a transition toward representative government, but the transition isn't guaranteed and can take a very long time. From the signing of the Magna Carta in 1215 it took nearly 500 years before the Glorious Revolution took place, leading to the Bill of Rights, which limited the power of the monarch and enforced regular elections.[12] [13] One hundred years later the American and French Revolutions represented the next big step in the spread of democracy but even then, it was stop-start.[14] [15] Democracy was a major threat to the ruling European elite and the people of France endured five separate invasions designed to restore the French monarchy. Even in France, males were given the right to vote in 1792 only to have this right revoked three years later. It was only subsequently reinstated after the revolution of 1848.[16]

In 1870, the fifteenth amendment to the US Constitution prohibited state and federal governments from denying any male citizen the right to vote due to "race, color, or previous condition of servitude." It was intended to further strengthen the rights and representation of African Americans.[17] But the amendment abolishing slavery five years earlier had been a significant blow to economically and politically privileged white Americans who were going to do what they could to hold onto their advantage. They introduced hurdles to voting, such as literacy tests and poll taxes from which white voters were exempt if they could show descent from someone who could vote. Literacy tests were administered by white officials with sole discretion to determine whether someone passed or failed. Questions included examples such as the following from a literacy test in Alabama; [18]

Question: "If a bill is passed by Congress and the President refuses to sign it and does not send it back to Congress in session within the specified period of time, is the bill defeated or does it become law?"

Answer: "It becomes law unless Congress adjourns before the expiration of 10 days."

These laws restricted the representation of African Americans in government. In 1896 there were 130,000 registered black voters in Louisiana, and by 1904 this had fallen to 1,342.[19] This lack of representation permitted the introduction and maintenance of further laws designed to segregate and restrict African Americans' access to education, employment and business opportunities and to ensure a continuing supply of cheap labour in the southern states for many decades after the official abolition of slavery.[20]

The Voting Rights Act of 1965 was signed into law by Lyndon B. Johnson and prohibited racial discrimination in voting practices, leading to a dramatic increase in voting and representation of not only black but other previously disenfranchised groups. [21] [22] Between 1965 and 1967 the percentage of African Americans registered to vote increased from 29% to 52%.[23] As with the 1870 passing of the fifteenth amendment, the Voting Rights Act was not the end of attempts to disenfranchise African Americans. In 1971 Richard Nixon's "war on drugs" initiated a steep rise in incarceration rates, resulting in a nearly five-fold increase by 2010. [24] [25] The war on drugs was politically motivated and intended to cement Nixon's image as a law and order president, but it also disproportionately impacted African Americans (probably intentionally). By 2010, drug offences made up 45% of all incarcerations and African American males were five times more likely to be incarcerated than white American males.[26] Most US states have laws that restrict ex-felons from voting, either temporarily or permanently. As of 2016, an estimated 7.4% of African Americans were banned from voting, compared to 1.8% of all other ethnic groups.[27]

Women have also historically had to fight for the right to vote. New Zealand is credited as the first country in the world to give women the right to vote in 1893.[28] It took until 1920 for the US to follow, and 1944 for France – 150 years after the French Revolution.[29] [30] The Swiss canton of Appenzell Innerrhoden held out on permitting women to vote on cantonal issues until 1990, while women in Saudi Arabia were first allowed to vote and run for office in 2015. [31] [32]

The right to vote is also no guarantee that your voice is likely to be heard or understood as well as others. In 2016, 61% of the US population were white – compared to 91% of US senators, only 24% of whom were female.[33] [34] And while most people get a vote, there are other factors which can cause even a democratically elected government to act against the wishes of the majority. In 2014 alone, 140 individuals donated over $500,000 each to US "super PACs", or political action committees that are permitted to take private, corporate and institutional donations and direct them towards influencing the outcome of US elections. The largest individual donor in this period contributed nearly US$100 million.[35] Individual donors and those individuals associated with the corporations and other institutions behind these donations might only get one vote, but there is no denying that they have a greater influence on election outcomes and on select politicians or political parties, than other, less financially well-off individuals.

Once democratic ideals and institutions become entrenched in the political landscape and power is spread across a range of groups and individuals, it becomes increasingly difficult for any one party to dominate the institution of government – but there are no guarantees. Countless democracies have descended into dictatorships. Plato's Republic expects democracy to degenerate into tyranny as an elected champion of the people becomes addicted to power and refuses to let it go.[36] German adult males have been able to vote since 1867, while women joined the vote in 1919.[37] In 1933, Hitler won 43% of the vote and formed government through a coalition between his National Socialists party and the German National People's Party.[38] Within two weeks the passage of the Enabling Act allowed Hitler to enact laws without the approval of the German parliament. Shortly thereafter, all other political parties were banned, and the National Socialists stood unopposed.[39]

Democracy requires a deep respect and commitment to rules, process and long, boring documents. Processes don't make us feel safe, proud, engaged or motivated like a strong leader or a superhero can. Hitler was a masterful orator, capable of both inspiring and terrifying. The people of Germany were struggling through a depression and war reparations that meant their quality of life was much worse than it had been 50 years prior. The promise of a return to former glory delivered by a charismatic leader to a population in crisis was enough to put Hitler into power and enable him to wipe-out over 60 years of democratic tradition, protections and infrastructure, in a matter of weeks.

Democracy reflects particularly human drivers and emotions. Many African nations are still dominated by strongmen leaders who influence their democratic processes in undemocratic ways. The Nehru-Ghandi family in India and the Bhutto family in Pakistan look more like royal dynasties than elected representatives.[40] This could be due to India and Pakistan having first embraced democracy only 70 years ago, during which time trust in the system has been gradually building, but the US declared independence from the British Commonwealth in 1776. The US Constitution was ratified in 1788 and is one of the most famous and revered documents in the world, next to specific religious texts. Yet despite over 200 years of democratic history and a population of nearly 330 million people from which to source the most qualified candidates, US voters gravitate toward political dynasties such as the Roosevelt, Kennedy, Bush, and Clinton families. In a society with the population of the US, it is highly unlikely that two or more people from the same family are actually the best qualified to hold some of the highest positions in the land, and yet voters support names they know – including relatives of former leaders, public figures, sports, TV and movie stars.

Winston Churchill referred to democracy as "the worst form of government except for all the others that have been tried from time to time."[43] It takes a long time for democracy to emerge, and even longer for it to approach being truly representative of the people it is supposed to represent. Once established there is no guarantee it will remain. But if we can get it – and keep it – it does come with one main advantage over some of those other forms of government.

Change

Dr Spock may have said it best when he said, "Change is the essential process of existence."[42] Without change we would still be whatever it was we were before the big bang coughed us up. It is constant change that has taken us from a point 13.8 billion years ago, when we were an assorted mix of quarks and other subatomic particles, to hydrogen atoms, all the way up the periodic table, to self-replicating protein strands, RNA, DNA, trillions of different organisms in between and then, to us. Without change, nothing (interesting) is possible.

Most other forms of government, like monarchies or dictatorships, tend to like things the way they are and are resistant to changes that could in any way threaten the status quo. Change is hardwired into the democratic process. It helps democracies to protect against the accumulation and abuse of power, but it also provides a mechanism for improving the process and performance of government. Opposition and aspiring political parties criticise governing parties on any perceived weaknesses in their policy platform. From general economic performance, spending or debt levels, down to individual policies. If voters are not happy with the performance of a politician or a political party, they can vote them out.

Each successive governing party has an opportunity to improve economic and other policies, including trying to find the right balance of chaos and control.

There are limits to the effectiveness of democratic change, however. Living organisms are subject to random mutations. Those mutations that improve an organism's chances of survival are more likely to be passed down to subsequent generations, gradually improving species' fitness over thousands and even millions of years. Businesses compete for survival by consciously experimenting with changes that they hope will improve their competitiveness in the business world. Over time these changes accumulate, leading to improvements in the products and services available to us. Democratic government takes a different evolutionary path. There are not multiple governments in a single environment competing for scarce resources, subject to selective forces and improving their performance over time through the application of either intentional or unintentional improvements. The only changes guaranteed to occur are those that are constitutionally mandated, such as through periodic elections. But elections do not necessarily result in change, as voters can elect to maintain the status quo – and not all democratic governments place term limits on representatives.

If voters do vote for change, they don't necessarily like all the policies championed by the party they vote for. When we go shopping, we can pick and choose which products we like from many different providers, but political parties offer a platform of policies and voters cannot pick and choose between individual policies they like. Instead, voters will generally consider which party's collection of policies is preferable to those of alternative parties. This will then be considered alongside things like the personalities or reputation of key members of the party and voters' membership or opposition to groups with a particular party preference. Voters are also subject to different biases which can reduce the importance of a party's actual policies. For example, studies have shown that confirmation bias plays a big part in voting practices.[43] [44] Confirmation bias is where we prefer sources of information which are in line with or confirm our existing beliefs or opinions. It ultimately arises from the desire to be right or smart. When we read information that agrees with our positions, we feel validated, we were right all along. Information that disagrees with our positions, suggests we might actually be wrong. Not only is it nicer to be right than wrong, if we are wrong, we might have to make changes. If we suddenly believe in climate change, we might start to think we should be driving a more efficient car. If we can't afford a new car, then our newly challenged belief might make us feel bad about the car we do drive. The longer we have held a particular belief, the more difficult it can be to let it go. If our parents and grandparents have always voted for a particular party, the implication of changing parties might be – simplistically - that they were wrong too. As a result, if voters hold a particular belief about a party or a policy, they will often seek out or preference information sources which confirm their beliefs rather than objectively reviewing a variety of information sources which would otherwise enable them to make a more informed decision. If voters believe that a minimum wage has a particular impact on economic growth, or that one or the other party is a more reliable economic steward, they will preference information that confirms rather than contradicts their beliefs, regardless of actual evidence on the matter. This issue appears to be exacerbated by the highly fractured modern media environment. Whatever belief we as individuals might hold, there is usually an information source which will confirm that belief. This all impacts the degree to which elections result in the implementation of superior economic policies.

Even where such biases can be avoided, it's not easy for either voters or policy makers to figure out what policies are likely to actually be of benefit. The government of one nation, state or city can be compared and criticised relative to another, but the complexity of government is such that it can be very difficult to isolate the overall benefits and disadvantages of one policy over another.[45]

In response to the global financial crisis and subsequent sovereign debt crises from 2007 to 2010 and beyond, countries across the world took different approaches in their fiscal and monetary policies.[46] [47] Some elected to implement huge stimulus programmes and others focused on fiscal austerity and cutting spending. The COVID pandemic was another global event that saw a range of different government responses; from enforcing strict lockdowns, to trying to maintain a balance between lockdowns and continuing economic activity.[48 49] These were governments of democratic nations, elected by populations that have similar wants and needs, all taking very different policy approaches to similar challenges. The idiosyncrasies and complexities of each nation make it very difficult, even with hindsight, to determine which nation's government chose the right or wrong response to these situations. This can make it difficult for policy makers to learn from their own experiences, and from each other. It is then even more difficult for voters to determine which party's policies are likely to be most beneficial when casting their vote.

If a product doesn't sell or a business makes too many poor decisions it will cease to exist. A government is unlikely to go out of existence. Voters are not silly; they are fully capable of casting out parties or politicians that are clearly incompetent economic stewards. Even if the party holds onto power, it may be with reduced seats or at a reduced margin, which might motivate the party to revisit unpopular policies. But there are many other issues that voters also consider. A political party could make the right decisions economically but disappoint voters on another key issue, like foreign or social policy. The reverse can also be true, a poor economic steward could remain in power because they are popular for a variety of other reasons. It could also be that the economy is performing well (or poorly) for reasons that have little to do with the current political party. One party could make all the right decisions and lessen the impact of a difficult period and still get the blame for it, while another makes poor decisions without reprimand because they were in power during a time of relatively strong growth.

Our institutions have a huge influence on our lives, with government the biggest and most powerful institution of all. In the absence of real-life superheroes, democracy restricts the degree to which power can be amassed or abused by a single, imperfect group or individual. It also helps to ensure that government continues to evolve towards better fulfilling the needs of the people. Its change mechanisms are an ungainly and imperfect, however. As a result, it can be a slow and sporadic process by which democratic government brings about real improvements to economic policy.

CHAPTER SEVEN

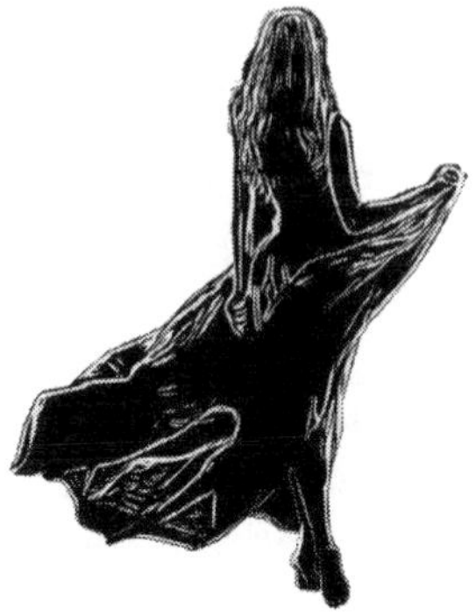

THE MATRIX

The Matrix is a simulated reality. Its inhabitants think they are living a normal life, oblivious to the fact they are sitting in transparent, goo-filled pods, their body heat used to power the sentient machines that have enslaved them.[1] The simulation needs to feel real. If it doesn't, the inhabitants become suspicious, rejecting their reality and either dying of despair or waking up and unplugging themselves. The Matrix is controlled by an architect and a series of programmes that manipulate its code to ensure that the humans inside remain oblivious to the real world. This is pretty much exactly how things work in the modern economy, or at least part of it anyway.

The modern economy's Matrix is money and the financial system. Money is the lens through which we perceive our economic reality. It is through the manipulation of money and the financial system that our economic architects manage our perception in an effort to keep us all plugged in, making our small, collectively invaluable contributions to the machine.

They might be doing us a favour though. Money is an essential component of the modern economic system. Like many other human innovations, it has played a big part in many people's ability to enjoy a privileged lifestyle in the modern world. It is quite difficult to imagine life without it, and like many great inventions, it's hard to wonder how we used to get by before it. Perhaps the primary thing that money does is enable us to confidently trade goods and services for something that we don't need, on the expectation that we will be able to trade the thing we don't need for something that we do. This sounds like a small thing, but it's because modern humans have always had this convenience.

Consider how hard it would be for us to get the things we need without money. The odds of finding someone who has what we want and who wants what we have, are low. Instead, we have to undertake a series of trades to go from what we have to what we ultimately want. Trade without money is an inconvenient, inefficient and costly way to get what we want.

With a form of currency that is readily accepted by all participants, we can pay money for the things we want, and the seller can use that same money to buy whatever they want. Because this does not require a series of inefficient trades the overall cost of the transaction is substantially less than what it would have been, meaning that we probably get more in exchange for our goods or our time.

Money is non-perishable, it doesn't rot or decay which means that you can hold onto it for as long as you like before spending it. There is also no need to concern ourselves with the quality of a dollar we receive. One dollar is worth the same as another.

Money is also divisible into small quantities, which means you can exchange some of it now for one or multiple things and put some aside for spending on something else later on. This divisibility further ensures that there is less wastage in the exchange of otherwise non-divisible items. With money, we can exchange things for the dollar or fraction of a dollar that they are worth to us. The trading parties must still agree on a price, but they are likely to arrive at a more mutually agreeable price when talking in dollars and cents than in clunky, non-divisible items.

A significant practical benefit of money is that it is usually small. There is no need to go to market with a trailer or a wheelbarrow, as a wallet or handbag will usually do the job. For the same reason it is also quite mobile (even before it became electronic). It would be very hard to enjoy, say, a round-the-world trip while paying your way with tradeable items.

Money that is widely used also provides the marketplace with a nice, universal measure that individuals can use to ascertain whether an item is worth buying or selling. Value is of course, subjective. Where two people might pay the same amount of money for an item, they are likely to place different values on the item, and one person may have been willing to pay significantly more than the other. Money is therefore not a measure of value as such, but it does provide buyers and sellers with a common language with which to communicate the "price" of a good. It is the code through which we all perceive and understand our economic worlds. Rather than quoting a price in numbers or fractions of a microwave or a chair, advertising the price in money brings all market participants back to the same reference point from which it is much easier to make a decision. No need for complex calculations, we just consider the monetary value of one thing (like an hours' work) with the monetary value of another thing (like a pizza), and we can quickly determine whether we're willing to make the trade. This reduces the complexity, effort and time required when undertaking a transaction and therefore also reduces the transaction costs, leaving more money to be spent on what we want.

From these simple yet profound contributions, money makes many additional benefits also possible. Money is suitable for saving, lending and borrowing. Other things can be saved, lent or borrowed as well of course, but the permanency and divisibility of money in a functioning economy provides people with confidence that working harder today and storing money will permit them to work less or to acquire more of what they want in the future. As a concept that follows on naturally from saving, money can be lent with confidence that it can be used in the future on its return (so long as it is paid back). Money makes the charging and calculation of interest also simple, and interest provides people with a reason to lend money, or in effect to lend that portion of their production that is beyond their own requirements. That in itself provides a reason for people to perhaps work a little longer and a little harder, with the knowledge that the benefit of their additional efforts doesn't mould, rot or otherwise go to waste. On the other side of the equation, money also facilitates some individuals being able to work less or have more of what they want or need today, while paying for it later.[2 3 4]

These simple functions have grown into an incredible mix of services and processes upon which the modern world and modern economies are wholly dependent. They facilitate the exchange of goods, services and labour, home loans and savings accounts, corporations or Kickstarter projects that leverage the surplus output of thousands or even millions of individuals to achieve many wondrous, hopefully world-bettering objectives. While people and their desires are likely to bring about growth all on their own, money, like language or the internet, makes the process a whole lot easier.

This is perhaps best demonstrated by what can happen

when money fails. At the onset of the French Revolution in 1789, the French National Assembly hoped to pull the fledgling government out of bankruptcy and began printing the Assignat, a bond issued against the value of properties recently confiscated from the Catholic church.[5] There were no controls on how many Assignats could be produced however. Excessive printing beyond the value of the assets they were intended to represent led to a collapse in their value. This resulted in massive price increases and economic turmoil. In response, the Maximum Price Act of 1793 was passed.[6] Merchants were required to post a table of the maximum prices that they could charge for their goods and were punished if they tried to charge more. They could be fined, imprisoned or even executed. Farmers, butchers, bakers and shopkeepers already dealing with wildly fluctuating prices brought on by excessive printing of the new Assignats were now unable to set prices that would adequately compensate them for their efforts and expenses. Most legislated prices were below the costs of production, so production plummeted. The economy disintegrated further, resulting in riots and food shortages and the death of thousands of people.

In December 1794, the law was finally repealed. The instigators of the law were themselves subsequently executed. The Maximum Price Act got the blame, but it was only deemed necessary due to the excessive amount of Assignats that had been created which led to massive price inflation. In 1800 the French central bank, Banque de France was founded by Napoleon Bonaparte and tasked with issuing a new, more stable currency, the Franc Germinal.[7]

It's only money

Historically, commodities with real value such as gold, silver, rice or shells have been used as a medium of exchange in preference to paper money.[8] Many nations today still retain copper coins as the lowest unit of money. These things have real value. A kilo of rice can keep you alive for a week. Today's money has virtually no intrinsic value. You can't eat a kilo of money. If it's the new age plastic money you probably can't even burn it safely to keep you warm. If push came to shove, a copper five cent piece is probably worth more than the €500 note. Money is only worth what somebody else is willing to give you for it. And what they're willing to give you for it is totally dependent on what they think they can get for it at some point in the future.

And then of course, what you can get for your money is totally dependent on what is being produced through the efforts and resources of the people around you. While money and the financial innovations that it permits are of immense value in facilitating and lubricating a functioning modern economy, its ultimate value is 100% dependent on individuals converting their efforts, time and resources into things that we might like to own or to trade for our own creations. This, on reflection, is totally obvious. It is also easily forgotten in a world where the most abundant and in-your-face thing in any economy, more so than any other feature, good or service, is money.

As a defining feature of all modern societies and an innovation that has emerged independently all over the world, money is probably about as definitively human as kissing and ball sports. Paper money is likely to have originally evolved from gold or other commodity-based money as a form of IOU, a promise to make good on an agreed trade or to provide the actual thing of value at some point in the future.[9] A trusted person goes to market and wants to buy something for which they haven't brought enough tradable goods. The seller might be willing to accept a piece of paper (or equivalent) with which the buyer commits to handing over the agreed amount of a commodity at some point in the future. If the issuer is regarded as particularly trustworthy, the seller might even be able to hand over this IOU as payment to a third party, another seller who also feels confident that they will be able to redeem the IOU when presenting it to the issuer. In this way, paper money can enter general circulation. If there are no real questions arising as to whether or not the paper can be exchanged for something of value, it becomes nearly as good as, and in many ways better, than the real assets that it represents.[10] [11]

The most trustworthy and therefore popular forms of paper money have traditionally been issued by banks like Banque de France. A bank's existence is dependent on the confidence of the people.[12] One of the simplest purposes of a bank is to keep people's assets safe. If you have accumulated wealth beyond what you are comfortable to lose or protect yourself, then a bank will hold onto it for you. If you deposit money with a bank, they guarantee to pay it back within an agreed time frame, perhaps on demand. Of course, banks exist to make a profit. If their only role was to keep people's money safe, they would have to charge a fee for that service. Many banks do offer that service, for example by charging a fee to access a safety deposit box under their guard. But for the most part, banks actually borrow money and pay depositors interest until they have to pay it back. This is really appealing for both sides. Depositors' money is relatively safe and accessible, and instead of paying a fee for their money to be protected, they actually receive a payment for lending the money to the bank. For their part, banks will seek to do something with the money they borrow from depositors, and which generates them a higher fee than what they are paying depositors. They do this by lending it to people, businesses or governments in the form of loans, mortgages, credit cards and other forms of credit and charging interest on those loans. If the interest they receive from lending the money out is higher than the interest they pay depositors (overall) then they make a profit.

While this arrangement is intended to benefit the bank, the depositor and the borrower, it also has a big impact on the health of the broader economy. If a person chooses to bury their savings in the backyard, then the benefit of their excess output is temporarily lost to the economic system. If they save their money in the bank, the bank can leverage this deposit by lending it to someone else. If the money they lend is ultimately deposited back into the banking system (after being used to buy a new car or swimming pool or whatever), then a portion of that money can then be lent out as well. For example, if the bank receives deposits of $1 million, they might need to keep 10% in reserve (for when some of the depositors want their money back) but they could then lend out the remaining $900,000 to someone else. Once the $900,000 comes back in as a deposit, they can lend $810,000 of that and so on. Ultimately, if everyone that receives the money the bank lends out deposits it back into the bank (the same or another bank) then an initial $1 million deposit can support the creation of an additional $9 million of economic activity.[13] [14] Money created in this way is referred to as endogenous money. It is money created within the system as a result of transactions between banks, borrowers and depositors.[15]

Banks must meet several obligations associated with this process. While most nations require banks to maintain an amount of cash or reserves on hand to cover withdrawals, some banks are allowed to determine their own reserve requirements. Whatever their reserve requirements, banks can generally choose to borrow the money that is held as reserves from someone else, like another bank, meaning they might not need to receive or hold a single dollar in deposits. They are required however, to ensure that the value of their overall assets is high enough that they will be able to repay all of their debts. For example, if the bank has $900 million in debt, then it might be required to have at least $1 billion of assets. This $100 million buffer is referred to as shareholder's equity.[16 17] It is the money that the owners of the bank, its shareholders, are ultimately entitled to if the bank were to be wound up. If the value of the bank's assets were to fall, the idea is that they would hopefully not fall below $900 million in value. This would result in the shareholders – who intentionally take on greater risk in the expectation of greater reward – losing some, or all of their money. But so long as the value of the bank's assets do not fall below $900 million, it should be in a position to pay back other investors, including people who have deposited money in the bank. If the value of the bank's assets were to fall below this amount and it was unable to repay depositors all of their money, then confidence in the banking system could be severely damaged. If depositors reacted by wanting to withdraw more money from other banks it could lead to a widescale run on banks and potentially to cascading bank failures. The failure of money, banks and the broader financial system would severely hinder an economy's capacity to leverage and multiply the benefit of each individual's output.

Pre-1907 in the United States, there was no central bank or body responsible for overseeing the financial system. Money was subject to laws of supply and demand, and it would flow east from New York in autumn to fund the Midwest harvests – if the New York financiers and industry wanted it back again, they had to pay for it with higher interest rates in the Winter. In 1906, a devastating earthquake destroyed 80% of San Francisco and absorbed a significant amount of additional funds for rebuilding efforts. Coming into October of 1907, the supply of money in New York was unusually tight. The earthquake and a number of recent overseas bank failures in Egypt, Japan, Germany and Chile meant that markets were nervous and US shares were already down 24% for the year. Within this fragile environment, on October 14 several key New York banking figures attempted to corner the market for shares in the United Copper Company. When their attempt dramatically failed, customers of associated banks who were concerned that their personal funds might have been impacted, began demanding the return of their deposits. Several banks and trust companies were running short on the required cash reserves to meet demand and on October 17 the State Savings Bank of Butte, Montana, announced its insolvency. Other banks that may have been in a position to help did not know which institutions were at risk of failure and were preoccupied with ensuring they themselves had sufficient liquid assets to meet increasing demand from their own depositors. Depositors demanded cash, banks were not lending to each other and were forced to liquidate assets to fund withdrawals – and as a result, the value of many of the assets that depositors' funds were ultimately invested in were also plummeting.

Within days numerous banks and trust companies had failed. Initially, depositors were withdrawing funds from stressed institutions and depositing them with other banks perceived as being more secure, but with every additional failure concern grew and the amount of funds deposited with other banks also fell.[18 19]

As of October 22, the next likely domino to fall was the Trust Company of America. The President of the Trust turned to archetypical US banker J.P. Morgan for help. Having decided during an emergency late-night audit that the firm ultimately held sufficient assets to cover its debt, Morgan declared, "This is the place to stop the trouble, then." The next night Morgan called the leaders of other banks and trust companies to an emergency meeting. He locked the door and refused to let anyone out until they had reached an agreement. With their support, together with the help of the US Treasurer, John D. Rockefeller, and ultimately US President Theodore Roosevelt, Morgan facilitated a range of initiatives that initially provided the Trust Company of America with sufficient cash to meet the demands of depositors, and which eventually restored confidence and convinced depositors to leave their money in the banks.[19 20 21]

Despite the prevention of an all-out financial collapse, a significant recession followed. Output in the US fell by over 10% and unemployment rose from less than 3% to 8%.[22] Without the intervention of Morgan and others the fallout from the crisis and the impact on the American people would have been significantly worse. The financial system was on fire and most people were running for the exits. Morgan knew however, that while some might make it out unscathed, most would not. By depositing money in banks that others were abandoning, by showing confidence and providing liquidity at a time when others panicked, they were able to reverse the swell of fear that might have otherwise decimated the US financial and banking system, and further damaged the economy.

There were no guarantees that Morgan or someone like him would be there to help coordinate a response to the next crisis and the financial system was too important to be at the mercy of earthquakes and speculators. In December 1913, President Woodrow Wilson signed the Federal Reserve Act and the US Federal Reserve System was founded.[23]

Initially, the goal of the Federal Reserve or "the Fed", was to prevent financial panics and bank runs by providing liquidity to its member banks. Unfortunately, sixteen years later, this strategy would prove to be insufficient. During the Great Depression, the Fed provided liquidity to those member banks that it deemed had sufficient assets to cover their liabilities. Many banks were not members of the Federal Reserve system at all and could not access emergency funds. In addition, the Fed required even member banks to attest that they had not lent money to brokers against speculative assets – many refused to do so.[24] While many banks still had access to the cash they needed to meet their requirements, those that didn't were forced to liquidate assets, increasing pressure on asset values that had already been falling since the beginning of the October 1929 stock market crash. Banks needed liquidity to meet the short term needs of depositors, but they also ultimately needed their assets to be worth more than their debts, or they would become technically insolvent. Beyond providing for member banks' liquidity needs, the Fed had lowered interest rates to close to zero to try and support lending, but many people, businesses and banks were trying to reduce their borrowings rather than increase them. Banks can create money by lending out a larger percentage of their reserves. If they reduce their lending, whether voluntarily to increase their reserves, or because fewer people want to borrow money, then they effectively shift from creating money, to destroying it. Increasing reserves may have helped some banks to fix their first problem - covering depositors' withdrawal requests, but it exacerbated their second problem - falling asset values were pushing them to the brink of insolvency.[24 25]

The Fed's Open Market Investment Committee was formed in 1923 and was the forerunner to the Federal Open Market Committee which was legislated in 1933. From its very first meeting the Committee had a focus on "the accommodation of commerce and business".[26] This focus would strengthen over time to include managing the supply of money and the health of the broader economy.[27] Unfortunately, its actions in the lead up to the Great

Depression would ultimately make matters worse to the point that its response in the aftermath was ineffectual. In 1928 the Fed began raising interest rates which contributed to the US economy weakening the following year. Rather than pausing rate rises, it continued raising rates into the recession to try and curb stock market speculation (which was likely to start unwinding soon anyway).[28] From 1928 to late 1929 rates were increased from 3.5% to 6%. By October 1929, the economy was already in decline, interest rates were up and money was harder to come by. The stock market began to crash in late October, losing 50% of its value by the middle of November. The Fed began lowering interest rates a week after the crash began.[29] [30]

In total about 7,000 banks failed. Between 1929 and 1932 the money supply fell by approximately one third and US property values dropped by approximately 67%. Shares lost approximately 80% of their value from peak to trough. The US economy shrunk in size by 30% and unemployment peaked at 25%. The economy would ultimately take about 10 years to recover.[31] [32]

Though it wasn't blamed at the time, the Fed's response is now seen as at least partly to blame for the economic and financial crisis that unfolded. Rising interest rates exacerbated both an economic slowdown and an asset price crash. Falling asset prices then undercut the Fed's liquidity measures, while rising unemployment and falling wages undercut the potential stimulus that might otherwise be provided by lower interest rates.

One of the foremost experts on the causes of the Great Depression is US economist, Ben Bernanke. In 2006 Bernanke became Chairman of the Federal Reserve. Shortly after he was instated, cracks once again started to appear in the US financial system. The Fed was caught in a cycle of lowering interest rates in response to economic and financial downturns which would support the excesses of the next cycle. Low interest rates in the late 1990s contributed to the dot com boom which deflated in 2000 and resulted in interest rates being lowered to levels not seen since the 1960s. This then contributed to a home lending boom which began to unravel after the Fed funds rate increased from 1% to 5.25% from 2004 to 2006.[33] From the mistakes made leading up to the Great Depression, Bernanke did not believe that it was the role of interest rates and the money supply to squash asset price booms, but he was ready to respond to the next big bust.[34] From July 2007 through to December 2008, the Fed lowered interest rates from 5.25% to effectively zero. Not only did it provide liquidity, it also bought assets that no-one else wanted including shares in the banks themselves in order to stop them from failing. It also facilitated stronger banks acquiring weaker banks which they would not have done without the Fed's financial support.[35] [36]

It probably could have done more to stop it from happening in the first place and was widely criticised for many aspects of its response. But with the lessons learned from its failed response to the Great Depression, the Fed helped to ensure that the fallout from what is often referred to as "the Great Recession" was significantly less damaging than what was seen during the Great Depression.[37] US unemployment peaked at just over 10% and GDP fell by 4.3% - the largest drop since the Second World War, but nothing on the 30% drop seen in the 1930s.[38] Even though 500 banks failed, this was also substantially less than the 9,000 that disappeared between 1929 and 1933 and they generally failed in an orderly fashion.[39] While millions of people lost their savings during the Great Depression, depositor losses during the Great Recession were zero.[40] [41] Bernanke and the Federal Reserve understood that saving banks and the financial system was dependent on saving the economy and vice versa.

Central banks' approach to maintaining confidence in the financial system continues to evolve. In 2012 the Fed formally switched to a policy of targeting a specific level of long run price increases or inflation within the economy along with maintaining employment and stable, long term interest rates. Inflation targeting was first introduced in New Zealand in 1990.[42] [43] It is where a central bank sets an interest rate designed to achieve a targeted level of general price increases or inflation (the Fed currently targets a long run average of 2%). Because prices are closely linked to economic growth and employment levels, trying to maintain a positive, but relatively low rate of inflation supports economic growth. A positive rate of inflation also encourages people not to delay their purchases, supporting the flow of money around the economy today.[44 45]

Because inflation can be objectively measured targeting a specific level of inflation helps to increase transparency and accountability. Once people have confidence that the central bank is committed to the target, they can anticipate how interest rates might change in the future based on something that is visible to them (prices of everyday goods and services). This helps people and businesses to make smarter financial decisions – they know that if prices are rising, usually as the result of a strong economy, then interest rates will go up. If prices are flat or falling, usually as a result of economic weakness, interest rates are likely to come down. Even before the central bank starts raising or lowering interest rates, the real economy knows it's coming and can self-regulate. The result is that central banks shouldn't need to change interest rates as much as they otherwise might which should reduce the volatility of the boom bust cycle. This approach has been credited with reducing economic and financial market volatility and contributing to long term economic growth.[46 47]

Greek tragedy

The European Central Bank (ECB) currently targets an inflation level of 2% but in 2001 when Greece swapped the drachma for the euro, it was targeting a variable rate of less than 2%. As with Asian currencies pegged to the US dollar in the mid-to-late 90s, this convinced investors that there was a much lower currency risk associated with investing in Greek assets. Beyond the benefits of a simple dollar peg, euro membership also reduced the perceived risk of default with investors holding the belief that the ECB and other euro nations would support each other in the event that they were unable to repay their debts. At the same time, Greece's relatively low per capita GDP, newly opened access to European markets and comparatively attractive investment returns convinced many investors that Greece was a great place to invest. In 1995, interest rates in Greece were over 18%, while interest rates in Germany were approximately 7%.[48 49] As interest rates fell across the globe over the next few years, the adjustment in Greece was dramatic. Anticipation of euro membership meant that by 2000 interest rates had fallen to approximately 6%.

While inflation targeting has significant advantages, it does have its weaknesses – it does not take into account changes in the price of assets, has no allowance for changes in the quality of goods and often excludes food and energy. While prices are usually linked to economic growth, it is not a perfect correlation. It also does not allow for differences in growth and performance between sectors, industries or even geographic regions. As such, the ECB sets an interest rate which anchors rates for Germany, Greece, France, Slovenia, Vatican City and 12 other euro nations.[50] This means that upon joining the euro, Greek interest rates moved in line with those of Germany, France and other more structurally advanced European economies. From 2000 to 2010, private debt in Greece as a percentage of GDP more than doubled.[51] In Germany it fell by 5% (although Germany's remained higher overall).[52] Most of the new money flowing into Greece was being lent by foreign banks, happy to increase their lending due to the perceived reduction in currency risk (as there was no longer a drachma to fall in value compared to the euro) and default risk (the ECB and other euro nations would bail them out).[53]

Increased lending facilitated a decline in the Greek current account (what they're selling versus what they're buying). They were able to increase what they were buying from other countries without having to increase their own output. Their current account deficit increased from 7.8% in 2001 to 14.9% in 2008.[54] The Greek government could do the same, increasing expenditure without increasing their revenues. Greece's fiscal deficit was approximately 4.1% when they joined the euro, and it ballooned out to a massive 15.1% in 2009.[55] [56]

Euro membership had another impact on Greece's decade. Under the drachma, Greece's fiscal and current account deficits would likely have been coupled with a decline in the value of their own currency. People would have been selling drachmas and buying other currencies, like the euro, to import whatever it was they wanted from the euro nations. The more they did this the cheaper the drachma would become and the more expensive the euro would have become in comparison. A real-world drachma to euro exchange rate would have deteriorated to the point that Greeks would be less likely, less able, to import now higher-priced products and services. At the same time, it would also make their own products and services more attractive to everyone else. Imports would decrease, exports would increase, and Greece would not have accumulated the amount of debt that it ultimately did. Euro membership therefore not only gave Greece access to cheap credit, it also distorted its economic activity – which further exacerbated its deficit and debt run up. An abundance of newly cheap money in Greece also led to big increases in asset values, and house prices almost doubled in value between 2000 and 2008.[57] It also helped wages to increase faster than any other European nation, further reducing the nation's competitiveness.

The effect in Germany was the exact opposite. While Greece was having its currency propped up and their interest rates held down through association with economically stronger nations, Germany's currency was being held down and its interest rates were probably higher than they otherwise would have been. House prices in Germany went sideways – or even declined – throughout the same period, while wages also declined. As a result, its already efficient and highly competitive economy became even more competitive. In 2000 Germany had a small current account deficit. By 2008 this had transformed into 6% surplus.[58]

The period between 2000 and 2008 was probably an exciting time to be living in Greece. Wages and asset prices were increasing, money was cheap and Greek purchasing power hadn't been as strong for a long time. Greece's GDP grew from USD130 billion in 2000 to USD354 billion in 2008, a massive 14% year on year increase.[59] They also celebrated the return of the Olympic games in 2004, 108 years after its first modern incarnation. Money manipulations may not have been the only factor to blame for the eventual crisis. Other similarly affected euro member nations did not suffer the same eventual fallout. The Greek government probably hadn't demonstrated the fiscal discipline necessary to qualify for euro membership in the first place. The Olympics and euro integration probably contributed to a rising tide of confidence, which itself further exacerbated everyone's appetite for risk (and everything else). Greek workers are sometimes stereotyped as lazy, living off the credit extended by other hardworking nations, but by hours worked, they are the hardest working people in all of Europe.[60] [61] Unfortunately, monetary distortions also contributed to them being the most indebted and up until the onset of the crisis, one of the least competitive in terms of prices for tradeable goods and services.

In 2010 with the impact of the financial crisis still reverberating, lenders began judging things such as debt and deficits more conservatively. They began to question previous assumptions that euro membership would protect them from default. As Greece's economic fundamentals were worse than most, the fallout there was severe. Greek government bonds plummeted in value with yields increasing from 5% at the end of 2009 to 35% just over two years later.[62] To try and restore confidence, the Greek government was forced to cut costs and raise taxes. In 2012 the minimum wage dropped 22%.[63] Between 2008 and 2013 unemployment rose from 8% to 27.5% with youth unemployment peaking at 60%.[64] [65] From 2008 to 2015 GDP fell from USD355 billion to USD195 billion, a 44% drop.[66]

Euro membership and ECB interest rate policy meant that the Greek economy, as perceived through the eyes of foreign investors, businesses, governments, and the people of Greece, was not actually real. It was a convincing simulation based on monetary and financial distortions that bore little resemblance to the real economy it concealed.

Money is used to modify, accentuate and distort economic reality. When the money supply is purposefully restricted during periods of economic strength, it is designed to make conditions more difficult for people than they otherwise would be. When there are reasons to be concerned economically, central bankers seek to make things easier, to convince us to continue to spend and behave as though there is absolutely nothing to worry about. Interest rates influences how much of it we spend, save, borrow and invest. Consequently, they impact all the activities or behaviours that are associated with those actions.

There's how much free cash we might have available to spend on other things after paying interest on credit cards, mortgages and personal loans etc. The interest rate also impacts the profits and losses a business makes, and whether they can afford to exist and give us a job or provide us a service in the first place. It impacts whether clients of the business can afford to buy its products and services and how much they are willing or able to pay for them. It equally impacts the cost of everything we buy, with the cost of money a component of the overall cost of production. In this way, manipulated interest rates can also act as a subsidy or tax. A car manufacturer in a low interest rate environment has a central bank-sponsored competitive advantage over a car manufacturer in a higher interest rate environment. This might be good in the short term but as with other subsidies it can induce practices or expectations in the low-rate environment, which would not be competitive or sustainable under higher rates.

The interest rate impacts demand and supply in goods and services, but it also dramatically impacts saving and investment decisions. When interest rates are low, we are less motivated to save and more motivated to borrow and spend - both as individuals and firms. When deciding whether to invest in starting or growing a business we assess the potential gains in line with both the costs and the alternative uses for the money. If we think a risky business venture has the potential to provide us with 10%

return on our investment and interest rates are 9%, we are less likely to invest as the cost of capital or the opportunity cost of investing elsewhere mean we can only make an additional 1% profit for a lot more risk than putting the money in the bank. If interest rates are only 2%, then the investment makes a lot more sense. As savers and investors, we might want at least 5% in order to delay our own spending in a low-risk or risk-free environment, but if bank interest rates are artificially kept at 2%, we might be forced to look for other, higher risk alternatives such as developing markets. Increased demand for riskier investments pushes up the prices of taking on more risk and simultaneously reduces returns. Across the board cheap money encourages increased spending, increased borrowing and increased risk taking.

The ultimate, obvious consequence of interest rates held artificially low over a period of time is that people, businesses and governments demand or borrow, and banks supply or lend more money than they otherwise might. People invest in things that they otherwise wouldn't; a bigger house, a new line of SUVs or an extra lane on a freeway. This supports economic activity and can be highly beneficial in the face of an economic downturn, but it can also lead to banks and borrowers lending or borrowing more than they may feel comfortable with in less economically favourable conditions.

Our economies would be nothing like they are today

without the huge advantages afforded by money and the financial system. We have also learnt many lessons which help us to enjoy the benefits they bring while mitigating some of their more challenging side effects. But for good and bad, money and the financial system misrepresent economic reality. In order for us to successfully navigate this simulated reality, we need to understand the role that money and the financial system play, but we also need to look past them to the real economy that they conceal.

CHAPTER EIGHT

THE DEFAULT SETTINGS

We often assume that even highly advanced lifeforms will have very similar concerns that elicit similar responses to our own. Most alien movies assume that extra-terrestrials will want something that we've got, and that they will use violence to get it – with little regard for our welfare or survival. Given our own history this may appear to be a reasonable assumption, but it may also be a little pessimistic.

The Zoo Hypothesis suggests that an alien species, having become aware of our existence, might spend a period of time observing us before choosing to reveal themselves and their mostly benevolent intentions. Any form of life that has mastered interstellar space travel has likely been in existence in an intellectually advanced form for a very long time. They would have many thousands – if not millions – of years of cultural and technological advancements behind them. They may have solved their own scarcity problem long ago and may simply be seeking the same thing that many travellers look for: a change of scenery. After a long existence in a relatively homogenous and disparate universe they may have come to appreciate the precious diversity that emerges from independent, living systems. They may also have come to realise that interacting with such a system can result in a less unique and precious form of hybrid. This is a very different scenario to what we have been led to fear and would suggest that our first alien encounter may be with something that is compelled not to attack or harm us, but to observe, interfering only where it helps to ensure our continuing existence and individuality.[1] It's also not without precedent in human history. Today there are over 100 "lost tribes" predominantly in South America, New Guinea and the Andaman Islands, whose isolation is largely protected by regional governments under a policy of non-interference to ensure their ongoing independence and right to self-determination.[2]

The way we respond to events, fears, challenges and opportunities is heavily influenced by a number of highly variable environmental, intellectual, cultural, philosophical and other influences. When Europeans came across new worlds in the fifteenth and sixteenth centuries, they had not yet reached a level of enlightenment and self-assurance that could be assumed to predate a philosophy of non-interference.

At the beginning of the sixteenth century, the feudal system was in broad decline following the devastation of the black death in the fourteenth century, which had caused the death of 30-60% of people in Europe.[3] [4] Deaths of lords, vassals and everyone else meant less infighting among nobles and a population that was more easily managed by a central ruler. The end of feudalism also meant the end of oaths of fealty and feudal fighting forces, resulting in a shift to professional, paid, centrally controlled armies.[5] Feudal forces, although loyal to king or queen, would not be expected to act against their own interests. Paid armies without ties to the region being governed could be directed more readily in accordance with a central ruler's wishes.

The Catholic Church wielded enormous power across Europe and had previously hindered localised or state-based concentrations of power, but it was a difficult period for them, too. In addition to the impact of the plague, the church was weakened by divisions and factional infighting epitomised by the early fifteenth century conflict known as the Western Schism; a forty-year period in which three separate individuals laid claim to the papacy.[6] Then, in 1517, Martin Luther published his Ninety-Five Theses, instigating the Reformation and further fracturing the church's power base – thus allowing regional monarchs, such as Henry VIII, to redefine themselves as head of both church and state.[7] [8]

Technology also played a significant role. The printing

press had been invented 70 years prior, and Martin Luther was able to spread his teachings across Europe to an increasingly literate public. The printing press and improved literacy rates also eased the administration required in larger empires, allowing rulers to dictate their orders via fewer intermediaries and misinterpretations.[9] Developments in artillery and other weaponry reduced the efficacy of protection provided by centuries-old castles and fortifications that had been crucial to the power of local aristocrats.[10] Knights, archers and soldiers previously valued for their years of training and experience could be brought down by someone with a few weeks training and a musket.[11] Increasingly, a local stronghold defended by a loyal, well-trained feudal force bound by tradition could be defeated by anyone with enough money to pay fighters and buy or produce modern guns.

More than ever before, a ruler's position was now maintained by gold and silver and developments in shipping, navigation and map making meant that new sources of both were within reach.[12] European economists from this period, collectively known as mercantilists, gave intellectual weight to this approach. They viewed the primary indicator of economic strength as a nation's store of silver and gold and logically, the greater the quantity of gold a nation controlled, the greater its capacity to cover the costs of any military engagement.[13] The result for the New World was the arrival of technologically advanced and aggressively expansionist forces hell-bent on extracting resources and building empires, without consideration of the impact on native peoples.[14 15]

While this was a devastating period for native populations of invaded lands, it wasn't necessarily great for many people back in Europe, either. The economy was important, not simply because it could improve the lives of its participants, but because of its capacity to help kings and queens expand and maintain their empires. Mercantilist theory focused on exporting as much and importing as little as possible to maximise a nation's balance of trade, and subsequently its reserves of silver and gold.[16] Domestic consumption was discouraged. The working class were a tool for maximising output, they would preferably be given just enough to keep them working and propagating (producing more workers) with any additional domestic consumption reducing the amount of goods available for export. [17] While workers were marginalised, many merchants thrived. They had a logical argument for exploiting the working class, while bans on imports meant they were not subject to foreign competition. Revenue arrived in state coffers predominantly via taxes and tariffs paid by the merchants and it was common for the state to grant monopoly rights to favoured groups or individuals to control and maintain revenue.

It took until the end of the eighteenth century for sentiment to begin to shift. Adam Smith, David Ricardo and others had begun pointing out some of the many flaws in mercantilist thinking. Silver and gold are not definitive measures of wealth.[18] The Aztecs may have had plenty of gold but that did not help them against Spanish steel, ships and horses.[15] Increasing the amount of gold in an economy also leads to drops in the price of gold and increases in the gold denominated price of other goods and services. The reverse would happen in those economies with falling gold reserves. There was a point therefore, where nations could gain greater benefit from paying or trading gold for other goods that they wished to import, rather than holding onto it. Merchants and others knew this and would often export or trade gold, against the wishes of the monarchy. In addition, the granting of monopolies and bans on imports stifled competition, reducing quality, innovation and technological advancement – which was further restrained by the fact that education of the working population was considered unnecessary (they were also, to be fair, probably too damn tired to do anything much other than work, eat and sleep).[19] [20] Resistance to trade also led to the domestic production of goods that could have been produced better and cheaper elsewhere. Domestic producers were rarely exposed to external competition and had to forgo potentially superior foreign inputs. The products that were available to consumers, including the government and the military, were rarely as good or as cheap as they could have been.

But the needs of the ruling class took precedence over those of lower classes. Rulers were dependent on gold and silver to maintain and expand their positions in a fractured political environment. The many individuals arguing in support of mercantilist principles didn't create this situation. Given they had the time, education and resources to write in favour of mercantilism they probably belonged to one of the groups that were benefiting from it, but that doesn't mean they were aware of its flaws. There was no central council responsible for the promotion of mercantilism. Some proponents may have been aware of its shortcomings, but protective of the advantages it provided them. Others, perhaps the majority, under the weight of a broad consensus probably just went with the flow and backed a seemingly solid intellectual argument aligned with prevailing ideologies and social and political realities. Mercantilist philosophy and associated policies emerged and dominated during this period because they were appropriate for the time.

Adam Smith began writing the Wealth of Nations in 1766.[21] [22] By this time the Scientific Revolution of Copernicus, Galileo and Newton had increased the focus on reason and empiricism, which in turn had fed into enlightenment philosophies and increased questioning of religious and political orthodoxies. Absolutism and the divine right of kings had received a literal blow with the 1649 execution of Charles I of England for effectively placing personal interest ahead of the good of the country.[23] The monarchy had been temporarily restored under Charles II but the Glorious Revolution in 1688 initiated a long and steady shift of power away from the

Crown to the British parliament, and ultimately the people of Britain.[24] At the same time, Britain was beginning to acknowledge the impact of the Industrial Revolution, which would demonstrate that the value of human effort and ingenuity could far surpass that of silver or gold. The Industrial Revolution brought about many innovations, but it also initiated a further fracturing of power. The British Parliament, which had consisted predominantly of landed nobles, was already more representative of the people than previous kings and queens, but it was still very much apart from the common man. The Industrial Revolution brought increased economic mobility and offered members of the lower classes a chance to join the elite, accelerating the division of wealth and power.[25]

The French Revolution did not occur until after publication of the Wealth of Nations, but its seed had already been sown by the middle of the eighteenth century. Its eventuation would further accelerate the deconstruction of the monarchy and the advancement of economic policy for the people.

Eventually it was the world wars that would mark the real end of colonialism and traditional imperialism. They significantly weakened imperialist nations, both militarily and economically. Colonies became increasingly difficult to control and resources were spread too thin.[26] Political and economic enemies also saw the benefit of sabotaging colonists' efforts by supporting target colonies either directly or with weapons, training and technology. Even superior military forces could no longer expect the one-sided victories experienced by the conquistadors in early battles against the Aztecs and the Mayans. The increasing costs and complexity of gaining and controlling colonies was beginning to outweigh the benefits.[27] The world wars also reminded European nations that they themselves were at risk of foreign invasion. Mercantilism saw imperialism as supporting a nation's survival. Yet it was one of Europe's least successful colonists, Germany, which was economically and militarily decimated from the first world war, which quickly emerged as the continent's biggest threat. At the same time, the emerging nuclear threat meant that the wrong war had the potential to bring devastation to anyone. Those who may previously have had something to gain now also had something to lose. With little apparent value to be gained from occupying or controlling other lands, and a real threat of being controlled or destroyed themselves, formerly imperialist sentiment suddenly shifted to the defence of the sanctity of a nation's sovereignty.

The world wars taught other valuable lessons. Forced reparations paid by Germany following its defeat in WWI contributed to its economic collapse, which paved the way for the rise of the Nazi party and ultimately WWII.[28] An economically destitute nation can be a dangerous one. As a result, the Marshall Plan instituted in 1948 sought not to punish but to support defeated nations.[29] This was an entirely different approach to post-war treaty negotiations, but one which saw the defeated nations experience significant economic growth and emerge as stable, contributing members of global society. These nations committed to ongoing peace, initially due to the embargoes placed on them in exchange for economic support, but also as a result of the deeply felt cost of the conflict and ultimate defeat.

The Great Depression, humanity's most global economic event at the time, further emphasised the fact that industrialisation, global trade and an increasingly interconnected financial system meant that your neighbour's economic plight would directly impact your own.[30] Suddenly, through economic and financial contagion but potentially through more direct political and potentially military measures, another nation's economic disturbance could directly influence the health of your own economy, and not, as the mercantilists thought, in a good way.

The first and second world wars also accelerated the continuing shift away from monarchist rule. The void left behind was filled with various ideologies and systems including fascism, communism and an increasing number of democracies. The subsequent drawn-out decline of purely communist nations further contributed to the continual increase in governments considering people's economic wellbeing when determining economic policy.

Just as mercantilism thrived when conditions were right, when its principles and logic aligned with the people who could endorse and promote them, the theories of Adam Smith and the classical economists took hold in a world that was ready to hear them. When we think that the logic of an argument for or against a certain economic policy is obvious or irrefutable, there's a fair chance that it fits within the default settings of our time. Our economy is inseparably intertwined with these settings. They impact how we perceive the world around us, our views on what is right, fair and just, how we treat each other and how our laws, institutions, financial and economic systems are structured. In turn, they are fundamental to the faith we have in these institutions and the extent to which they augment or repress our innate capabilities. Most modern societies and economies are worlds away from mercantilist Europe, the Soviet Union or North Korea. They are generally founded on principles like participatory and representative government, equality under the law and personal and economic freedoms. However, underneath these broad definitions are large variations in the cultural and institutional landscape. Economic policies and decisions are largely restricted to travelling the paths and inhabiting the spaces defined by this landscape.

Today's settings

Today's landscape has similarities and differences to every other that has gone before it. What really matters, what's really having an impact, is unlikely to be obvious for years to come, but right now a few things are apparent.

After the lessons and losses of the two world wars, punctuated by the horrors of Hiroshima and Nagasaki, global politics became all about the power balance between the US and the USSR. After the fall of the Soviet Union, it appeared that the US would be the world's only superpower for the foreseeable future – but its power and influence has declined for a number of reasons.[31 32] While the US still has the world's most powerful military, recent conflicts have shown just how quickly it can be stretched to ineffectiveness.[33] Multiple prolonged and expensive conflicts, coupled with economic turmoil through the global financial crisis, have also contributed to a shift in US focus from global activism to internal, domestic matters.[34] At the same time, other rising powers and centres of influence such as China, Russia, the European Union and the United Nations have become increasingly active.[35 36]

Global politics is becoming increasingly complex, but this does not necessarily mean an increasing likelihood of major international conflicts. The expansion of personal freedoms and participatory government over the last 70 years means that military action increasingly requires the support of the soldiers, their families, and the people whose day-to-day lives, economic wellbeing, freedom of movement and sense of security will be impacted.

The nuclear threat has also likely led to a reduction in major conflicts due to how abhorrent full-scale – or any-scale – nuclear conflict is likely to be. The cold war saw two world powers fighting to win global support for diametrically opposed political philosophies. One was democratic and fully engaged in the global economy. The other had not had a vote in a generation, lost 20 million people to the second world war and could have had its entire research and production effort focused on winning a war – but still, thankfully, they both thought better of dropping the bomb.

The spread of technology, global alliances, trade in modern military equipment and increasing wealth and investment in the military means that many nations without nuclear capabilities are a long way from being considered superpowers but still maintain militaries capable of withstanding or doing considerable damage and deterring even the most powerful opponents. Multiple messy and prolonged conflicts throughout the twentieth century between military-powerful nations and poor, relatively ill-equipped forces have shown that no military action is without significant consequence for both sides.[33]

Russia's continuing, but so far less-than-successful invasion of the Ukraine has shown the importance of trade, not just in military equipment but also in ordinary goods and services. Without trade, most nations would struggle to maintain a sufficient supply of weapons and equipment necessary to sustain an intensive, prolonged invasion while shortages of other goods and services are likely to reduce support for the conflict.[37] At the same time, international support for the Ukraine has helped it to resist and even humble a militarily superior force. If a nation is democratic, economically open and dependent on strong military or economic partners it is less likely to be willing or able to fight anything other than a quick and decisive conflict or one with strong domestic and international support.

Political globalisation has also seen the rising influence of global institutions and networks. The United Nations, European Union, World Trade Organisation, International Monetary Fund, and global corporations, economic, trade and other groups, are increasingly determining or impacting policies in all areas of life. These groups are coordinating responses to globally and regionally significant issues such as major conflicts, climate change, forced displacement of large groups of people, issues in global trade and finance and wide scale human rights abuses.[38] They are also influencing more mundane aspects of our day-to-day lives such as labour laws, intellectual property protection and privacy.[39] [40] In the same way that national governments align policies within borders, the impact of these institutions is an increasing alignment of policies across national borders and wider regions.

Even bilateral trade agreements are contributing to the alignment of policy, as trade partners are requiring more of each other than a simple reduction of tariffs, government interference and open access to markets. A key issue at the heart of the US/China trade war was the Chinese government's failure to take adequate steps to protect US companies' intellectual property rights.[41] As part of a 2019 trade agreement, the EU brought about a significant improvement in fuel quality in Australia. Petrol used in Australian cars was among the dirtiest in the world and the worst of all developed countries due to high levels of sulphur. In negotiating the agreement, the EU required Australia to improve fuel quality to allow for increased imports of cleaner-burning European cars. Consequently, the Australian government was forced to bring forward plans to improve fuel quality, likely leading to a significant reduction in Australia's CO2 emissions.[42] In addition to pushing for a positive impact on climate, EU trade agreements increasingly require trading partners to respect considerations such as enforcement of democratic principles, the rule of law and human rights.[43]

As of 2019, corporations operating in more than one country were responsible for approximately one half of global trade and one third of global GDP.[44] Corporations are subject to rules and regulations that often transcend borders, either as a matter of legislation or of internal policy.[45] The Foreign Corrupt Practices Act (FCPA) introduced in the US in 1977 made it unlawful to bribe a foreign official, after approximately 400 US companies admitted to making over US$300 million in payments to representatives of foreign governments and political parties.[46] [47] While enforcement and penalties in the foreign jurisdiction may be weak, the legal and reputational risk at home reduces the instances of corrupt practices abroad, and not just those perpetrated by US citizens. Similar standards such as the UK Bribery Act and the OECD Anti Bribery Convention require individuals and corporations to abide by local laws internationally, effectively exporting and improving standards from one jurisdiction to another.[48] [49] The FCPA and similar rules and regulations often extend requirements to foreign based customers, suppliers and partners, and cover topics such as corporate governance, labour laws and discrimination.

Globalisation is not just about large, traditional institutions. The internet and social media have also facilitated significant grassroots movements including the #MeToo and School Strike for Climate, which have impacted both attitudes and policy.[50] [51] Such movements, made up of geographic and culturally diverse groups, are responding to shared experiences across geographic boundaries. They are facilitated by technology, by open democratic governments that ensure people's right to free speech and an independent media – and also due to the fact that more and more of us are, literally, speaking the same language.

Some estimates suggest that 90% of the 7,000 languages in use today will die out within the next 100 years.[52] [53] While this is bad from a cultural and linguistic perspective, it is gradually making it easier for the people speaking the remaining languages to understand each other. It's estimated that approximately 5 billion people, or 65% of the world's population, speak one of the world's ten most widely spoken languages– with up to 20% of people able to speak English and an estimated 60% of the 10 million most popular websites presented in English.[54] [55] The percentage of websites in English is reducing, but this is generally due to big increases in the percentage of websites in one of the other top ten languages, as speakers' use of the internet increases. Whatever the language, translation tools are making it easier for people to navigate language barriers, both virtually and face to face.[56] Regardless of what happens with an individual language, improvements in education, translation tools, and the requirements of global commerce, tourism and intertwined institutions will likely continue to increase the degree to which we understand each other.

Beyond language, our understanding of each other is improving in other ways. New technologies and applications and an explosion of media and information sources has enabled isolated individuals or minority groups to connect with others who understand them. Individuals who felt they did not belong, or that their experiences or opinions were not shared or valued by the people around them, are now forming groups with influence. These groups are often supported by others who have previously felt that they also have not been heard.

Close to 50% of the world's population lives under

democratic government.[57] [58] This compares to just 10% before the end of the second world war. It's not simply that more nations are turning to democracy, as long-standing democracies are also becoming more democratic and more representative of the people they are charged to govern. Minority and other previously underrepresented groups are playing an increasing role in public institutions, government and corporate boards. Increased representation brings increased attention to the needs and concerns of these groups, and ultimately to a wider proportion of the population.

Over the past 60 years, as the number of democratic governments has tripled, global GDP has increased ten-fold. The number of people living in extreme poverty, defined as living on resources worth less than US$1.90 per day declined from nearly 2 billion in 1990 to 736 million in 2018.[59] This was during a period in which global population increased by approximately 2.5 billion people. Up until the COVID pandemic, it was estimated that the global "middle class" was increasing by approximately 150 million people each year – that is, their income was increasing to the point where they have some level of discretionary income. They can afford things like mobile phones, motorbikes, movie tickets or maybe a vacation somewhere. They may not be rich, but they're also not days away from starvation. This is likely the first time in human history that so many people find themselves in this position.[60] [61]

Democracy and a gradual increase in the distribution of wealth have increased focus on things that benefit the broader populace, like education, healthcare, safety and infrastructure. At the end of World War II approximately half of the globe was illiterate, but today the figure is below 15%.[62] Average global life expectancy was 46 years in 1950, and today it is 73.[63] Prior to 1900 nearly half of all children globally died before their fifteenth birthday, in 1950 it was 27%, today it is below 5%.[64] An increasingly powerful lower and middle class are using their resources, their voices and their vote to increase their chances of improving their economic wellbeing and maintain their trajectory out of poverty.

Another core contributor to this positive feedback loop is the increasing contribution that women are making to the global economy.[65] When women are educated and engaged in formal employment, economies grow, infant mortality falls, and children's overall outcomes improve. Education and employment opportunities for women also lead to a reduction in birth rates, as women have alternative life choices available to them.[66] When the birth rate drops the smaller number of children receive a greater investment of both time and resources from both the increasingly educated mother and father, further improving future prospects for both girls and boys. It has been estimated that about half of the economic growth experienced by OECD countries over the past 50 years has come from improvements to education and employment opportunities for women. Developing nations that have improved educational and employment opportunities for women and girls have led emerging market growth rates in recent years.[67]

Through improving health and education, broader participation in economic activity and politics, and increasing levels of wealth, people's lives are generally improving. At the same time, due to increased immigration, cheaper travel, global media, largely open and accessible internet, global trade and a convergence of political systems, we are becoming more aware of each other and more alike than ever before. There's a good chance that we drive the same car, eat at a similar restaurant chain or watch the same movies as a stranger living half a world away. At a deeper level, our forms of governance, living standards and key measures of wellbeing are gradually converging. Every day, despite being greater in number than ever before, people on the planet are becoming safer, smarter, healthier, richer, more alike and in many ways more connected.

These positive developments are a cause for celebration, but not all current default settings are positive.

The not so good

If 50% of the global population are not living in poverty, then 50% still are. The COVID pandemic has actually contributed to the first increase in the number of people living in extreme poverty in a generation.[68] While this is hopefully only a temporary reversal, most of these people will likely still live and die poor. Poverty is less of an issue in developed countries, but it remains a persistent problem. Since 1970 the percentage of people living in poverty in the United States has stubbornly ranged between 10% and 15%. The actual number living in poverty has steadily increased in line with growth in the US population.[69] In most cases poverty in developed nations is not what it used to be, nor is it as debilitating as in less developed nations. Many developed countries use definitions of poverty that account for overall increases in wealth and which link to a percentage of median income that is also increasing over time.[70] Most people in developed nations have access to food, housing, education and healthcare, but the disparities between upper and lower classes are still considerable.

On some levels it may not matter if the rich get richer, so long as everyone else's wellbeing is also improving – but on other levels it matters a lot. People compare themselves against others in their community, region or country before considering how their situation stacks up against someone in another country or another time. Research from Daniel Kuhlmann, for example, found that people are less satisfied with their own house if their neighbour’s house is bigger, regardless of the size of their own house.[71] A further study from researchers at Purdue University suggested that happiness increases up to a certain level of income, but beyond this level the positive effects of increased wealth are offset by pressure to earn more as earners compare themselves against other high earners.[72] Increases in wealth among people we come into contact with contribute to dissatisfaction with our own lives as we become aware of the things they have that we don't. There may be poorer people somewhere else in the world and our ancestors may have had a tougher time of it than us, but what we feel and respond to the most is how we compare to our peers and our neighbours.

IMF research suggests that high levels of economic inequality increase the likelihood of social unrest and that social unrest can impact economic growth which often worsens inequality, setting off a "vicious cycle".[73][74]. While absolute poverty may be of greater concern, relative poverty and high levels of income and wealth disparity in the developed world can feed dissatisfaction and negatively impact social cohesion.[75] Globalisation, for example, brings significant benefit to global and regional economies, but it can also disrupt industries, employment and income in impacted sectors. This can contribute to greater levels of inequality and disparities within nations, while still contributing to a reduction in disparities between nations. Globalisation may lift aggregate wealth, but by doing so in a way that often exacerbates local in-country inequalities it has been – and remains – controversial.[76]

Income disparities are usually further exacerbated during times of economic uncertainty. Economic downturns have an outsized impact on the poor and middle classes, who are less likely to have sufficient reserves to enable them to maintain their lifestyle in the face of job losses or lost income from small businesses. Hope is a significant driver in our sense of wellbeing. If we expect our situation to improve, we feel substantially better about life than if we expect our situation to get worse, regardless of the position we find ourselves in at present. The opposite is also true. Economic downturns and a pessimistic outlook further contribute to social unrest, which increases the desire for change. Social networks and fragmented media can help us find like-minded and empathetic groups or individuals, but they can also amplify and leverage fears and frustration, polarise opinions and increase anxiety levels.[77]

We are in a period of significant economic turmoil today. The impacts of the Great Recession followed by sovereign debt crises had barely subsided before the onset of the COVID pandemic. The pandemic has had a huge impact on the day-to-day lives of people from almost every country across the globe. There is the fear of the virus itself, economic uncertainty associated with both individual and institutional responses to the pandemic, the loss of millions of lives, the toll on workers in healthcare and other essential sectors, plus the everyday burdens of lockdowns, home-schooling, missed loved ones, curtailed plans and lost time.[78]

It has put a hold – or at least a dampener – on the long-term trend toward increased global interconnectedness and interdependence.[79] Nations have been putting up figurative and literal walls to try to control the spread of the virus, but it has also highlighted risks associated with this interdependence. Hoarding and interruptions to primary, manufacturing and service industries, as well as constraints on supply chains, both local and international, have demonstrated just how close we can be, at any one point in time, to running out of the things we need. Practically, shortages, panic buying and strangled global supply chains may lead to an understandable focus on national and regional self-sufficiency which is not a bad thing.[80] A robust and diverse local economy can reduce the likelihood, extent and social cost of downturns, provide diverse employment opportunities, and reduce the environmental impact of shipping. If not managed effectively, however, an overemphasis on self-sufficiency can also create actual inefficiencies and higher costs for goods and services while feeding nationalist sentiment.[81]

The pandemic is not yet over, and its full consequences are still to be realised. Broadly speaking, the institutional response has mirrored a war time response with a massive increase in spending and welfare payments. As a consequence, government debt and deficit levels have increased to historic highs across the world.[82] But this spending, combined with measures to reduce the spread of the virus and improve access to care, probably eased the already terrible personal, social and economic costs of the pandemic.

While the pandemic has led to a huge reduction in

international and domestic travel for business and pleasure, there have been more refugees on the move in the last few years than at any time since the end of World War II. In 2019, there were an estimated 26 million refugees in different parts of the world, including the Middle East, Africa, Asia and South America.[83]

But this number could be dwarfed in the next 30 years thanks to the other massive challenge of our time – climate change. It's estimated that climate change could lead to the forced migration of as many as 1.2 billion people by 2050.[84] Much of the rest of the world will be dealing with an increased frequency and severity of natural disasters that include fires and floods, and changes in weather and climate patterns will threaten food and water security. Making the changes necessary to limit climate change and to spare us from the worst of its impacts is probably the single biggest collective challenge humanity has ever faced.

These challenges are contributing to political and social unrest, which can be a force for positive change, but which also creates an environment ripe for reactionary, polarising policies that may be appealing in many ways, but which aren't necessarily appropriate for the challenges faced. Economic uncertainty, income and wealth disparities, protectionism and nationalist sentiment can also increase the risk of regional and global conflict.[85] [86] The US has seen the limits of even the world's most powerful military force. At the same time, other global powers like China are keen to benefit from their increasing power and influence. These and other nations are at risk of responding to domestic issues in unhelpful ways that could result in regional or possibly even global conflict. The degree to which this will improve as the pandemic recedes and other global trends play out is unclear.

There have certainly been worse times for most of the world's population to be alive, and the robustness of human economies means that, even now, most of us still have jobs, food and somewhere to live. But during times of uncertainty the world can change and respond in uncertain ways. Sometimes for the better and sometimes for the worse.

The ultimate default setting

Adam Smith said that man is an anxious animal.[87] Regardless of our physical reality, we tend to feel some degree of anxiety. Historically, as a species we've never really been able to relax for too long. During our millions of years of existence in a genetically similar form, the chances of us making it from conception to old age were very, very low. We're anxious because we've had good reason to be. Our bodies and brains have not caught up to our safer reality, reduced likelihood of calamity and other characteristics that come with modern existence. They're probably not going to for thousands of years. When, or if they do, that will likely be the end of us.

Our anxiety, fear, greed, hunger, jealousy, love, lust and other most basic drivers continue to underpin the socio-cultural, political, economic and other settings prevailing at any one time, for better or worse. They drive continual progress and solutions to our problems, such as developments in social and physical technologies that have resulted in refinement of democratic processes, the development of multilateral organisations and advancements in healthcare, telecommunications, agriculture, and almost all other areas of our existence.

We are constantly seeking improvements, but enhancements in social technologies are difficult to isolate, test, refine and further improve. No two societies can be considered directly comparable, and results cannot be replicated or clearly attributed. The impact of social changes takes time and what and why something has the impact it does will change over time. Beyond issues of measuring the impact of change, individuals and groups struggle to agree even on what constitutes positive change. Some want higher GDP, others want more even distribution of wealth, some want increased government, others to reduce it. Within the uncertainty and complexity surrounding these changes each group can generally find facts – or at least a passionate argument – to support their interpretation. How likely each group's argument is to be accepted is then heavily influenced by the theoretical currents and crosswinds prevailing at the time.

Theoretical Foundations

Economics is a robust field of study. We undoubtedly understand more about how an economy functions today than we have at any time in the past. This understanding crosses over into complementary and overlapping specialisations such as psychology, finance, sociology, anthropology, political science and other areas. But economics is not a hard science. It is a soft science dependent on other soft sciences. This is not an insult. At the centre of the soft sciences are human beings. And for as long as we have observed and studied humanity, we have known that human behaviour is incredibly difficult to predict. This is true for the individuals we interact with on a day-to-day basis, and even more so when attempting to understand the behaviour of strangers within groups within larger groups acting within complex institutional frameworks.

Figuring out what's going on in an economy is so difficult that the 2021 Nobel Prize in Economics was awarded not just because of what recipients had discovered, but how they discovered it. David Card, Joshua Angrist and Guido Imbens won the award for using "natural experiments" – observing the impact of economic policies in the real world, where conditions allowed for the testing of hypotheses using a form of natural experiment and control groups.[88] Natural experiments can be very valuable and provide insights that can't be replicated in mathematical models, but it's also hard to isolate the specific variables economists are studying, and other factors can skew or obscure the results. They can also be very difficult to replicate in a manner that would be sufficiently similar to clearly support or contradict earlier findings. This is very different to other hard sciences, which can hypothesise, test and retest theories until they can be confidently relied upon in the real world or as a foundation for further studies.

This inherent difficulty in establishing a clear theoretical basis, combined with the interplay between economics, philosophy, politics and other disciplines, means that it can be difficult to achieve a stable theoretical consensus upon which economic policy can be built. For example, John Maynard Keynes began arguing for the value of counter-cyclical government deficit spending to moderate economic downturns as early as the 1920s.[89] It is a widely accepted response to economic downturns to the extent that responses to the COVID-induced downturn nearly 100 years later almost unanimously incorporated elements of this theory. It seems to work, and yet we've spent about a hundred years fighting over it.

The immediate response of the US central bank and federal government at the onset of the Great Depression was widely considered to be the opposite of Keynes' recommended course of action. The Federal Reserve allowed the money supply to drop while increasing banks' reserve requirements (after allowing many banks to fail altogether), while the government increased taxes and initially only marginally increased spending. Sweden was the first country to successfully and intentionally use deficit spending to improve economic conditions, in 1934.[54] While other national, state and local governments followed with their own spending and recovery plans, they were mostly funded by new or increased taxes. Ultimately, it was spending in response to the second world war that increased economic output and gave rise to the unfortunate term, "Military Keynesianism".[91]

After the second world war, China and other nations incorporated into the Soviet bloc adopted a Marxist-Leninist approach to communism.[92] Other nations not sold on communism, looked for a form of democracy that would deliver a better post-war world. For countries such as Britain, France, Italy and the Nordic nations, this was "Democratic Socialism".[93] Democratic Socialism retained significant free-market elements and it was underpinned by a democratic process, but it involved extensive government intervention including infrastructure spending, welfare programmes, support for labour movements and nationalisation of key industries. While Keynesianism was only part of Democratic Socialism, its principles were part of the justification for an even deeper government involvement into economic activity than Keynes' had originally recommended.

In 1973, the energy crisis brought sky-rocketing oil prices, oil and petrol shortages and widespread inflation. Deficit spending was designed to stimulate demand, but it was of limited use against supply-driven shocks and even exacerbated the issue as increased spending and increased money supply further fuelled inflation.[94] By the late 1970s, inflation and interest rates were too high, nationalised industries had become increasingly uncompetitive and government expenditures and deficits had blown out to concerning levels.[95] On top of this, the early success of the Soviet bloc was fading and China was being torn apart by the cultural revolution and failed attempts to control its economy. Increasingly, anything considered communist, socialist or even just leftist, was deemed to have failed.

Keynesianism became synonymous with increasing government controls, spending and debt.[96] Margaret Thatcher and Ronald Reagan on the other hand, became the new champions of classical economics and the invisible hand, reducing taxes, government controls, spending, and debt (at least in theory).[97] Thatcher had some success in reducing government spending, reducing union influences and improving competitiveness and efficiency in the economy, but she also oversaw a doubling of the number of unemployed and significant increases in poverty levels and income inequality. Britain also endured two recessions under her stewardship.[98] Reagan's presidency is largely considered an economic success, but his approach wasn't entirely anti-Keynesian. During his two terms as President the US federal government ran up higher deficits and debt levels than most of the presidents who came immediately before or after, including Democrats Bill Clinton and Barrack Obama.[99] [100] Neither Thatcher nor Reagan's leadership or economic records could be regarded as conclusive evidence for or against countercyclical deficit spending, but their perceived success in countering Democratic Socialist policies more generally put them at the centre of the resistance to Keynesian policy.

In the twenty-first century, fiscal responses to the Great Recession reflected the level of disagreement. The Great Recession and its aftermath saw investment losses, tightening of lending and financial markets, and spiralling increases in unemployment that resulted in collapsing demand for goods and services. Government responses varied between austerity (reducing government spending and debt) and massive stimulus programmes.[101] [102] It was a classic case for Keynesian spending programmes, but many nations, particularly in Europe, believed they did not have the money to spend. Some were probably right. The sovereign debt crisis revealed that Greece and other nations could not afford to spend their way out of the recession (particularly while tied to the euro). However, much of the rest of Europe only resorted to significant deficit spending on bond buying programmes after seeing how this benefited other nations – such as the US – that had committed to this path.

In 2020 and 2021, many nations had debt to GDP ratios as high or higher than it was during the Great Recession or the sovereign debt crisis, but the COVID-induced economic crisis was something different.[103] Initially, it wasn't clear how supply chains were going to hold up, whether essential industries and services were going to continue to function, or the extent to which many sectors would be able to adapt to the new realities. Unemployment sky-rocketed and the people who did keep their jobs didn't know how long they were going to be able to do so. The uncertainty, drop in confidence and falls in output were largely unprecedented. Perhaps because of these factors, there was little question about what government could *afford* to do. It had a massive role to play, not just in trying to limit the spread of the virus and ensure the continuation of essential services, but also in limiting, as best as possible, the precipitous fall in economic activity.[104] [105]

Some Keynesian concepts are hardwired into most modern economies. Automatic stabilisers such as marginal income tax, unemployment benefits and other welfare payments have the effect of reducing taxation, increasing government outlays during economic downturns and reducing them during periods of strong economic growth. Politicians like lowering taxes and spending money, and deficit spending is an easy way to do that. It can also be practically difficult to limit it to downturns, particularly for infrastructure projects, for example, which can take years to complete. But these are not shortcomings of the theory. Whether someone associates an economic theory or policy with socialism, capitalism or even communism does not mean it is automatically a good or a bad policy. The expectation that the government of a sovereign nation should be able to control its spending in the good times in order to maintain its capacity to support demand in downturns, or that a government may use Keynesian theory to justify its own endless expansion is not a shortcoming of countercyclical deficit spending. It is a shortcoming of the government employing it. But this can be difficult to separate from the theory itself.

We are currently about as close to uniform consensus on the value of countercyclical spending as we've probably ever been. But like mercantilism, classical economics and so many economic theories or frameworks, this consensus is subject to continuous pressure and changing realities which mean that it will likely be up for debate again sometime soon.

An economy is an emergent property of its host society. Each society has its own natural environment, history, culture, physical infrastructures, institutions, and underpinning theories. No two societies will be exactly alike, and neither will any two economies. Mercantilist societies had a very different set of priorities to those of most democratic societies today. Even these more similar, modern, democratic societies have their own unique characteristics and objectives. What we can expect from our economies and what economic policies best suit a society's goals and objectives will always vary depending on the relevant default settings.

CHAPTER NINE

BETTER REPLICANTS

Replicants are bioengineered humanoids that are so advanced it's almost impossible to tell them apart from actual humans. In fact, the only way to tell is through a series of increasingly emotive questions or statements referred to as the Voight-Kampff test, which is designed to betray a Replicant's inhuman status. It includes questions or statements like; "You're watching television. Suddenly you realize there's a wasp crawling on your arm." Or; "Can you remember being in love? How did it make you feel?"[1 2] Real humans respond to the questions with emotions like happiness, joy, sadness, fear, shame or disgust. Some questions are designed to elicit a mild response, others a strong response. While the Replicants can usually pick the correct emotion, they might not be able to judge the intensity of emotion the question is expected to elicit. They might also struggle to comprehend that not all humans will have the same response and that over many questions, each human would be expected to reveal their own unique set of fears, triggers and desires.

Our economic models are a type of artificial intelligence that attempts to mimic a real-world economy – or a part of it. They can appear to be reasonable imitations of reality, and they can, at times, provide valuable information on how a real economy might respond to a particular policy or change. These models are limited by practical constraints like computing power. But they are also limited by our capacity to define all the potentially relevant factors and their interrelationships, from the underlying default settings, human and societal considerations, and institutional, political and financial market responses. As a result, we usually don't try to take all these considerations into account but focus instead on a limited set of inputs and outputs.

There are certainly some things that we have a pretty good feel for. Monetary policy, for example, is quite formulaic and rule based. It also seeks to impact usually only one or two metrics (inflation and possibly growth or employment) by adjusting a single input (the interest rate). This makes it relatively easy to model. We can be relatively confident that increasing the interest rate will reduce the amount of money being borrowed and increase the amount of money being saved, which will reduce demand for goods and lead to falling prices, or at least slow the rate of price growth (and vice versa). We can track this rate of change closely (albeit retrospectively) and have a single mechanism (mostly) for adjusting it. Because it is widely accepted that central banks should be free to act independently, there is also much less political interference, removing another complicating factor. There are also lots of central banks across the world that have been following a similar playbook, each a natural experiment with similar goals but small variations in approach and outcome that contribute to our understanding of what works and what doesn't. Monetary policy is far from simple and far from perfect, but its rule-based nature, singular focus, limited policy options and relative independence from outside influence make it easier to model than many other components of the economy.

Elsewhere, most policy decisions must take into account many more inputs and outputs, including shifting goals, political considerations and unique default settings. This added complexity limits the usefulness of lab-built models and the applicability of what has or hasn't worked in the past, which can make it hard to determine the likely impact of potential changes or policy options.[3] For example…

Minimum wages are bad for the economy

The traditional model of wage policy suggests that wage flexibility contributes to economic growth. Minimum wages should be avoided or kept very low as they restrict the economy from finding a natural equilibrium and can increase unemployment, particularly during economic downturns.[4] [5] For example, some employers might be happy to pay, and some workers might be willing to accept $8 an hour. If the minimum wage is set at $10 an hour, then these jobs won't materialise, and unemployment will be higher than it otherwise would be with fully flexible wages. As wages are also part of the cost of most goods and services, higher wages also increase the cost of production or provision of those goods and services, which could make them more expensive than those of competitors or competing economies which pay lower wages.[6] [7]

Greece's minimum wage grew about 5% a year from when they joined the euro in 2001, to the onset of the economic crisis in 2010. These increases initially appeared sustainable through the prism of a growing economy. But one of Greece's key advantages prior to these increases, and prior to joining the euro, was that their labour costs were much lower than those in much of the rest of Europe. The economic growth that followed was primarily a factor of inflated asset prices underpinned by massive increases in public and private debt.[8] Higher minimum wages, particularly of government employees, contribute to higher government expenditures and debt.[9] They also meant that the advantage that came from lower comparative labour costs, had eroded over time.[10] Minimum wages were part of the problem that led to

Greece's sovereign debt crisis and the economic crisis that followed, including massive increases in unemployment.[11] The minimum wage was ultimately reduced by 20% and has not returned to its peak over ten years later.[12]

If a minimum wage is set at a level substantially lower than employers and employees would otherwise agree to anyway, then it probably doesn't have any real impact. But if it is close to, or higher than this amount, then there is clear logic to suggest that it will be bad for employment and the economy.

Except when it's not

David Card's Nobel prize was awarded for a study in which he and his partner, Alan Kruger, suggested that even this apparent truism did not capture the full story. Card and Kruger's study looked at the actual impact of an 18% increase in the minimum wage in New Jersey and its impact on employment levels there, compared to employment levels in neighbouring Pennsylvania, which was very similar in most key respects, but did not see an increase in the minimum wage. Their finding was that, despite the significant increase, employment levels were not negatively impacted, and in fact, they actually increased after the wage rise.[13]

One of the key arguments against a minimum wage is that in an economic downturn, there is a limit to the degree to which wages can fall, in which case employers have no choice other than to cut staff and thereby increase the number of unemployed. As a result, a minimum wage can exacerbate economic downturns and make it difficult for the economy to recover. Flexible wages, like flexible prices, do enable an economy to adjust, but a minimum wage itself is likely to have only very minimal impact on the economy. Jobs and employees are not commodities or stocks that can be instantly and continuously traded without consequence. There are costs to the employer in letting go of workers.[14] They may have to pay severance packages and cash out unused holidays. They may also be letting go of people with expert knowledge in one or more aspects of their business, potentially impacting quality or productivity. If the downturn is short lived and they subsequently need to increase staffing levels, they will have to pay advertising, recruitment and training costs. There will likely be a period of reduced quality or productivity until new staff are as proficient in their roles as those who were let go. This can impact client relationships or the business's reputation and revenues in a way that has nothing to do with economic downturns. A reputation for making sudden and dramatic staff changes may make both retained and new employees feel less secure, and result in the business struggling to attract quality staff or having to pay a premium to get the people it wants.

For similar reasons, most businesses would be very cautious to shift wages in response to changes in economic activity unless absolutely necessary. Flexible wages go both ways. If employers expected to be able to drop wages during downturns, workers would understandably argue that wages should be quickly increased during periods of strong performance. But just like their employees, employers need to have some consistency in their revenues and expenses. Salaries are often flexible to a degree, either through bonus or revenue related payments, but in most industries these flexible payments make up only a small percentage of employee wages.

There is value in employers offering a stable wage that ensures employees receive a stable income and that employers have predictable expenses, as well as a stable and happy workforce.[15] This also reflects the fact that business owners and salaried employees often have very different goals and perspectives on risk. Business owners are often willing to take a higher level of risk in the hope of receiving an outsized reward. Salaried employees tend to place higher value on stability and consistency of income. Perhaps employers could pay less and maybe employees could get more in a fully flexible labour market, but the stress, cost, inconvenience and risk are often not worth it. This is not a factor of artificially fixed wages, but of the way employers and employees choose to interact.[16]

There is an absolute floor to a wage at which people just won't take the job. And it's not because they're lazy, greedy or ungrateful, it's because if a job doesn't pay enough to enable someone to feed their family, keep them warm and safe, and fulfil their most basic needs, they will be forced to do something different. That may simply mean getting a different job, but at the extreme it may mean waves of refugees abandoning their family and even their ancestral homes, willing to do anything or go anywhere to improve their lives. Fast food restaurants in New Jersey or Pennsylvania might not contribute to the refugee crisis, but before wages get complicated by academic studies or government policy, they are about the exchange of labour, offered willingly in exchange for resources that facilitate an individual's survival.

Separate to defining an actual "minimum wage", most economies have laws that even inadvertently contribute to a floor for wages.[17] Restrictions on immigration mean that there is a cap on the supply of labour. This also contributes to a relatively uniform expectation on the minimum standard of living an individual is likely to demand for their time. People also have limitations on what they're willing to do to achieve that minimum standard.[18] Despite the rise of remote work, many jobs and most low paid jobs still require workers to be physically present. That means that employers need to pay enough that workers can live within a reasonable distance from the workplace. Local, state and national governments tend to employ a lot of people and obviously pay salaries of their own. The wages they pay contribute to expectations as to what constitutes a living wage and appropriate lifestyle. If they themselves set salaries too low, then nobody will work for them. If they set them significantly higher than the minimum, then they can contribute to public perception that private sector wages are too low which leads to a "spill over effect", where higher wages in one sector or region contribute to higher wages in another.[19]

Even without these measures, as we become more prosperous we tend to prioritise a minimum standard of living that we are willing to collectively provide for. The minimums can vary substantially from country to country, but most developed nations have an expectation that people should not starve or freeze to death, or die from an easily treatable or preventable disease, even if they can't work at all. Over time, we tend to expect more from the minimum, including that working full time in any job should entitle you to enjoy at least some of basic comforts that others might take for granted, like a mobile phone, a comfy sofa and a Netflix subscription, maybe dinner out once every few weeks and the occasional holiday. As the average standard of living improves, our expectations of the minimum, whether that's for ourselves or someone else, tends to also increase.

If achieving this is not possible, there tend to be other costs to a society; people may reduce their costs or supplement their income in ways that aren't necessarily legal, even if just by engaging in the black market to avoid income or consumption taxes. They may be forced to stop spending money on things that end up costing themselves and society in other ways. They may not have the time or the money to further educate themselves, to move to an area with more or better jobs, or to transition to an industry or sector with better prospects. They may not have the time or the money to go to the gym, buy healthy food or live in an area close to parks or the beach. This can negatively impact their mental and physical health, which represents a further cost to themselves and their community.

There may be other reasons to work for a low wage, like pride, or building experience, but this can be offset by all the other things individuals can do to improve their situation if they don't have to work, like starting a business or improving their education. The costs and benefits of these alternatives, including expenses, lost wages and opportunity costs, can further reduce the attractiveness of the low wage job and are each heavily influenced by laws and policies of their own.

Where there is no minimum or the defined minimum does not allow for the above considerations, an actual minimum will emerge as a result of these many related – and sometimes seemingly unrelated – decisions. The introduction or change of a legislated minimum wage will likely have an impact on employment and the economy, but it is only one relatively stable factor among many other shifting considerations.

Greece did have a policy of increasing the minimum wage up until 2010. But this policy probably didn't mean much. Lenders perceived the Greek government to be much less likely to default on its sovereign debt once they were part of the euro with interest rates governed by the European Central Bank. This led to a big drop in interest rates paid by both the public and private sector, and a huge increase in borrowings. All the extra cash that was pumped into the economy was going to lead to higher wages regardless of any formal wage policy.[20] If the drachma was still in use or if Greece had been kicked out or elected to leave the euro, the drachma would have plummeted in value. Nominal wages would have remained the same while becoming increasingly competitive due to the shifting exchange rate. But continuing euro membership meant that a greater focus, and greater blame, was placed on the minimum wage policy itself. A minimum wage is intended to contribute to a minimum standard of living for its recipients and their families. What constitutes an acceptable minimum changes over place and time. In mercantilist England the minimum was simply whatever would keep workers alive, working and reproducing the next generation of workers.[21] The minimum standard has a floor based on what the economy can actually support. If wages shift too high and an economy becomes less competitive then the overall economy may shrink as a result. This can increase unemployment and, depending on the other support measures in place, result in real suffering.

If a society wants to prioritise a higher standard of living for low paid workers, there are lots of ways it can go about it. It could reduce their taxes or increase available benefits or welfare payments. It could implement policies designed to lower prices or remove sales tax from essential goods or services that low paid workers spend a significant portion of their income on. It could choose to offer some services, like childcare, for free, enabling people to work and earn more if they choose to. It could also choose to introduce or increase the minimum wage.

Despite the excitement, New Jersey's fast-food restaurants probably had less to worry about in 1992 than the nation of Greece in 2010. There's lots of possible reasons that wage increases in New Jersey resulted in more – or at least the same – number of jobs and that restaurant owners were able to increase prices enough to cover wage increases without impacting sales or profits. It may simply have been that the policy was just right. That is, enough of an increase to improve the quality of life of low paid workers and not so much that it resulted in job losses, or an exodus of customers or fast-food establishments.

It could also be that a minimum wage is both good and bad over different time frames. Research suggests that the negative impact of a minimum wage only emerges over time due to the time taken to impact an industry's competitiveness.[22] Other research suggests that minimum wage is beneficial over time in that it encourages capital investment towards improving efficiencies as well as increased spending on R&D, all designed to improve efficiencies and reduce reliance on the now more expensive workforce.[23] [24] In which case, while it might not be bad for the economy, it also might not benefit lower paid workers in the way it might be intended.

Depending on your political leaning and the default settings and peculiarities of the time and place, the introduction or increase of a minimum wage could be symptomatic of the insidious creep of paternalistic, leftist economic policy ultimately destined to morally and economically bankrupt us all – or it could be a shot in the war against capitalism, a small win for the proletariat along the march towards socialisation of the means of production – but it's probably neither of those. It's most likely one of many policies intended to contribute to a society's ever-changing objectives. It probably won't do quite as much good or as much damage as either side expects.

Both the traditional model and Card and Kruger's findings provide valuable insights into the impact a minimum wage can have on employment levels and the broader economy. But even the most considered and intricate models are no match for the complex reality they seek to understand and emulate.

We need economic theories and models to better understand our economy and to ensure that it continues to benefit us all, but until our replicants are much more advanced than they are today, it's important that we recognise their limitations.

CHAPTER TEN

THE FUTURE

We are born with fears and desires that drive our behaviours. We have certain mental and physical capacities which we apply toward getting the things we want and avoiding the things we fear. We are not alone but assisted by people who love and support us in accordance with their own fears and desires. Beyond these individuals are many millions of strangers who each play a small part in our survival. These strangers might like us if they knew us. If they heard about it, they'd probably feel sad if our homes were destroyed by a tornado and it would probably upset them if they saw us being hit by a bus. Many of these people would even generously give up some small comfort if it would in some way alleviate our suffering. Aside from that, however, whether we wither or prosper probably isn't of much interest to them, they have their own problems to worry about. They support us not because they care deeply about our survival, but because we happen to be part of a very complex and remarkably efficient system that converts human desires, theirs, and ours, into the things that fulfil them. We must have immense faith in this system because in our reliance on it we forgo a large degree of our own autonomy, and our capacity to survive without it.

It is not just the efforts of people alive and working today that support us. The system is built on a foundation of knowledge and both physical and social technologies that have been built up over the course of many thousands of years by people who have come before us. Some of these advances have had significant impact in isolation, but mostly they have propelled us forward with small, incremental and individually unremarkable improvements in our understanding and control of our environment. Money, which is one of these technologies, though not overly ingenious in its own right, has become synonymous with economic activity, significantly easing its facilitation while often distorting its true nature.

Without the benefit of our many social technologies we would never have ventured out beyond the confines of our innately defined social groups and subsequently beyond the fate decided for us by our surroundings. Yet this transition, while giving us greater control over many things, has increasingly put us at the mercy of our own institutions. These institutions can make our lives easier if we are lucky, or a whole lot harder if we are not. One of the ways our progress is hindered is by an inappropriate balance of chaos and control. The degree to which we can support each other to achieve our goals is reduced where controls are insufficient. Too many controls can stifle individual motivations and the benefits provided by continuous change.

Today, approximately half of the world's population live in societies in which they can influence these institutions and the rules and laws which they themselves must abide by. We try to push these institutions to change in ways that are of benefit to us, but that change is sporadic. It can also be very hard to agree on what we want or how to get it.

What we value as individuals and as a society also changes over time. While we continue to work to improve our understanding of how the economy works, with so much variation between economies and with societies and economies changing over time, it can be hard to determine the best way for a society to achieve its shifting economic goals.

There are obviously many other aspects to understanding economics and what drives an economy than what has been covered in this book. Someone living in a developed, democratic society might be more focused on things like supporting growth in the STEM sector, automation of industry or increasing their nation's share of the knowledge industry. They may not think that hunger, mirror neurons, Leon Trotsky or Somali warlords have much to do with their economy. For someone living in a developing nation these things may seem more relevant, but they might also be more focused on raising literacy levels or increasing the percentage of women in paid work. But responses to these challenges or opportunities must be considered in the context of the fundamental forces driving our economy. This includes our humanity, culture, institutions, government and financial systems, together with situational factors including the dominant theoretical frameworks upon which each nation's economy is based. If we want to understand the impact that a certain change or policy might have, why something isn't working the way we might have expected or how to make things better, we need to consider how it will likely interact with these factors.

Our economy is immensely valuable and without it, many of us literally wouldn't survive. It supports us to pursue our desires and provides most of us with a standard of safety and comfort that our ancestors could only dream of. It is also incredibly complex. Because of this complexity it can be difficult to predict the impact of even small changes.

One day, in a future imagined in science fiction books, we may develop a near perfect understanding of how the economy works. We may have filled both the gaps in our knowledge and the process by which we agree what constitutes 'better' in a way that benefits the majority, if not all of us. We might then be in a position to overcome our own scarcity problem and be ready to explore the universe for fun, not profit. This is probably a while off, though. For now, we continue working to improve our understanding of economics – while supplementing what we don't know with a little bit of science fiction where necessary.

The economy is a creature of our own creation. It is incredibly powerful and can be of immense benefit to us all – if we only look after it.

REFERENCES

Chapter 1

[1] Roddenberry G. et al., Star Trek, the Original Series. Hollywood, Calif., CBS DVD, 2008.

[2] Shelley M. Frankenstein. Lackington, Hughes, Harding, Mavor & Jones; 1818.

[3] Mill J.S. Inaugural Address Delivered to the University of St Andrews. 1867.

Chapter 2

[1] Overbye D. The flip side of optimism about life on other planets. The New York Times. 2015. https://www.nytimes.com/2015/08/04/science/space/the-flip-side-of-optimism-about-life-on-other-planets.html.

[2] Burchell M.J. W(h)ither the Drake equation? International Journal of Astrobiology. 2006; 5(3): 243–250.

[3] Department for Work and Pensions, Differences in life expectancy between those aged 20, 50 and 80 – in 2011 and at birth. https://assets.publishing.service.gov.uk/government/uploads/system/uploads/attachment_data/file/223114/diffs_life_expectancy_20_50_80.pdf.

[4] Social Security Administration, Period Life Table, 2019, as used in the 2022 Trustees Report. Social Security. https://www.ssa.gov/oact/STATS/table4c6.html.

[5] Carrier D.R., Kapoor A.K., Kimura T., et al. The energetic paradox of human running and hominid evolution [and comments and reply]. Current Anthropology.1984; 25(4): 483-495.

[6] Herculano-Houzel S. The Human Advantage: A New Understanding of How Our Brain Became Remarkable. The MIT Press; 2016.

[7] Mink J.W., Blumenschine R.J., Adams DB. Ratio of central

nervous system to body metabolism in vertebrates: its constancy and functional basis. American Journal of Physiology, 1981; 241(3): 203-212.

[8] Steiner P. Brain fuel utilization in the developing brain. Annals of Nutrition and Metabolism. 2019; 75(1): 8-18.

[9] Tseng J., Poppenk J. Brain meta-state transitions demarcate thoughts across task contexts exposing the mental noise of trait neuroticism. Nature Communications. 2020; 11(3480).

[10] Radford T. How we recognise faces. The Guardian. 2004. https://www.theguardian.com /uk/2004/dec/13/sciencenews.research.

[11] Institute of Physical and Chemical Research (Riken). Largest neuronal network simulation achieved using K computer. Riken. 2013. https://www.riken.jp/en/news_pubs/research _news/pr/2013/20130802_1/.

[12] Bird D.W., Bird R.B., Codding B.F., Zeenad D.W. Variability in the organization and size of hunter-gatherer groups: Foragers do not live in small-scale societies. Journal of Human Evolution. 2019; 131: 96-108.

[13] Dunbar R.I.M. Neocortex size as a constraint on group size in primates. Journal of Human Evolution, 1992; 22(6): 469–493

[14] Johnson S. Where Good Ideas Come From: The Natural History of Innovation. Riverhead Books; 2010.

[15] Keysers C. The Empathic Brain: How the Discovery of Mirror Neurons Changes our Understanding of Human Nature. Social Brain Press; 2011.

[16] Harsanyi J.C. On the rationality postulates underlying the theory of cooperative games. The Journal of Conflict Resolution. 1961; 5 (2): 179–196.

[17] Koenigs, M., Daniel T. Irrational economic decision-making after ventromedial prefrontal damage: Evidence from the ultimatum

game. Journal of Neuroscience. 2007; 27 (4): 951–956.

[18] Gale J., Binmore K.G. Samuelson L. Learning to be imperfect: The ultimatum game. Games and Economic Behavior. 1995; 8: 56–90.

[19] Nicholson N. How hardwired is human behavior? Harvard Business Review. 1998; 76, 134-147.

[20] The Bushmen Who Had the Whole Work-Life Thing Figured Out. The New York Times. 2017.

[21] Van Gelder L. A hunter's story. The New York Times. 2000. https://www.nytimes.com/2000/09/29/movies/film-in-review-the-great-dance.html.

[22] Diamond J.M. The Worst Mistake in the History of the Human Race. Oplopanax Publishing; 2010.

[23] Kinealy C. This Great Calamity. Gill & Macmillan; 1994

[24] O'Neill J.R. The Irish Potato Famine. Abdo Publishing; 2009.

[25] Dawkins R. The Selfish Gene. 2nd ed. United Kingdom: Oxford University Press; 1989.

[26] Leibeseder B. A critical review on the concept of social technology. Socialines Technologijos/Social Technology. 2011; 7: 24.

[27] Henderson C.R. The scope of social technology. The American Journal of Sociology.1901; 6(4): 465-486.

[28] Brooks A.S., Yellen J.E., Potts R., Behrensmeyer A.K., Deino A.L., Leslie D.E., Ambrose S.H., Ferguson J.R., d'Errico F., Zipkin A.M., Whittaker S., Post J., Veatch E.G., Foecke K., Clarke J.B., Long-distance stone transport and pigment use in the earliest Middle Stone Age. Science.2018; 360(6384): 90-94

[29] Dixon J.E., Cann J.R., & Renfrew C. (1968). Obsidian and the Origins of Trade. Scientific American.1968; 218(3), 38–47

[30] Smith K.N. New Guinea villagers unearth evidence of the island's Neolithic past. Ars Technica. 2020. https://arstechnica.com/science/2020/04/new-guinea-villagers-unearth-evidence-of-the-islands-neolithic-past/.

[31] Kelly R.L. The lifeways of hunter-gatherers: the foraging spectrum. Cambridge University Press; 2013.

[32] Ember C.R. Hunter-gatherers (Foragers). HRAF Explaining Human Culture. 2020. https://hraf.yale.edu/ehc/summaries/hunter-gatherers?print=print.

[33] Abramov I., Gordon J., Feldman O., Chavarga A. Sex and Vision I: Spatio-temporal Resolution. Biology of Sex Differences. 2012; 3(20)

[34] Abramov I., Gordon J., Feldman O., Chavarga A. Sex and Vision II: Color Appearance of Monochromatic Lights. Biology of Sex Differences. 2012 3(21)

[35] Ricardo D. On the Principles of Political Economy and Taxation. John Murray; 1821.

[36] Costinot, A., Donaldson, D. Ricardo's theory of comparative advantage: old idea, new evidence. American Economic Review. 2012; 102(3): 453-58.

[37] Mäki U. Aspects of realism about economics. Theoria. Revista de Teoría, Historia y Fundamentos de la Ciencia. 1988; 13(2): 301-319.

[38] Mäki U. On the method of isolation in economics. Poznan Studies in the Philosophy of the Sciences and the Humanities. 1992; 26(4): 317-351.

[39] Reynolds C. Flocks, herds, and schools: a distributed behavioural model. Computer graphics.1987; 21: 25-34

[40] Campbell R.H., Skinner A.S., eds. The wealth of nations. In Smith A. The Glasgow edition of the Works and Correspondence of Adam Smith Vol. 2a. Liberty Classics.1976; 456.

[41] Wightman W.P.D., Bryce J.C., Ross I.S., eds. Essays on Philosophical Subjects: With Dugald Stewart's `Account of Adam Smith'. In Smith A. The Glasgow edition of the Works and Correspondence of Adam Smith, vol. 3. Clarendon Press.1980; 49.

[42] Egyptian reed pen Archived. Wayback Machine. 2007. http://www.lib.umich.edu/pap/exhibits/writing/reed_pen.html

[43] "pen." The Hutchinson Unabridged Encyclopedia with Atlas and Weather guide. Abington: Helicon; 2010.

[44] How does a ballpoint pen work? Engineering. HowStuffWorks. 1998–2007. http://science.howstuffworks.com/question683.htm

[45] Liden D. Grain Production in China, 1950-1970: A case study in political communication. Asian Survey. 1975; 15(6): 510-529.

[46] Bottelier P. Economic Policy Making In China (1949–2016): The Role of Economists. Routledge; 2018: 131.

[47] Pantsov A.V., Levine, S.I. Mao: The Real Story. Simon & Schuster; 2013: 574.

[48] King G. The Silence that Preceded China's Great Leap into Famine. Smithsonian. September 26, 2012. https://www.smithsonianmag.com/history/the-silence-that-preceded-chinas-great-leap-into-famine-51898077/

[49] Spence J. Mao Zedong. Penguin Lives. New York: Viking Press; 1999.

[50] Chang G.H., Wen G.J. Communal Dining and the Chinese Famine of 1958-1961. Economic Development and Cultural Change, 1997; 46(1): 1-34.

[51] Meng X., Qian N., Yared P. The Institutional Causes of the China's Great Famine, 1959-1961. Review of Economic Studies, 2015; 82: 1568-1611.

[52] Becker J. Hungry Ghosts: Mao's Secret Famine. Holt Paperbacks; 1998.

[53] Akbar A. Mao's Great Leap Forward 'killed 45 million in four years. London: The Independent; 2010: 333.

[54] Long T., Leipe C., Jin G., et al. The early history of wheat in China from 14C dating and Bayesian chronological modelling". Nature Plants. 2018 (5): 272–279.

[55] Maddison A. Contours of the World Economy 1-2030 AD: Essays in Macro-Economic History. Oxford University Press: 2007.

[56] Working time required to buy one Big Mac in selected cities around the world in 2018. Statista, https://www.statista.com/statistics/275235/big-mac-worldwide-cities-working-time/

Chapter 3

[1] BenYishay A., Pearlman S. Crime and microenterprise growth: evidence from Mexico. World Dev. 2014; 56: 139–152.

[2] BenYishay A., Pearlman S. Homicide and work: the impact of Mexico's drug war on labor market participation. Working paper. Vassar College. 2013.

[3] Coronado R., Saucedo E. Drug-related violence in Mexico and its effects on employment. Empirical Economics. 2019; 57(2): 653-681.

[4] Schotter A. Free market economics. St. Martin's Press Incorporated; 1985.

[5] Ludvigson S.C., Consumer Confidence and Consumer Spending. Journal of Economic Perspectives. 2004; 18(2): 29-50

[6] Horowitz J.M., Brown A., Minkin R. A year into the pandemic, long-term financial impact weighs heavily on many Americans. 2021. https://www.pewresearch.org/social-trends/2021/03/05/a-year-into-the-pandemic-long-term-financial-impact-weighs-heavily-on-many-americans/.

[7] Gunnigle P., Lavelle J., Monaghan S. Weathering the storm? Multinational companies and human resource management through the global financial crisis. International Journal of Manpower. 2013; 34(3): 214-231

[8] McDonnell A., Burgess J. The impact of the global financial crisis on managing employees. International Journal of Manpower. 2013;34(3):184-197.

[9] Zagelmeyer S., Heckmann M., Kettner A. Management responses to the global financial crisis in Germany: Adjustment mechanisms at establishment level. The International Journal of Human Resource Management. 2012; 23(16): 3355-3374.

[10] Rapsomanikis G. The economic lives of smallholder farmers: An analysis based on household data from nine countries. Rome: Food and Agriculture Organization of the United Nations; 2015.

[11] Heathcote J., Perri F. Wealth and volatility. The Review of Economic Studies. 2015; 85(4): 2173-2213.

[12] Alessandrini D. (2021), Progressive Taxation and Economic Stability*. Scand. J. of Economics. 2021; 123: 422-452.

[13] Makin A.J., Layton, A. The global fiscal response to COVID-19: Risks and repercussions. Economic Analysis and Policy. 2021; 69: 340-349

[14] Ahrens S. Fiscal responses to the financial crisis. Kiel Policy Brief. 2009;11.

[15] Adrian T., Natalucci F. COVID-19 Crisis Poses Threat to Financial Stability. IMF blog. Posted 2020.

[16] von Wachter T. Lost generations: long-term effects of the COVID-19 crisis on job losers and labour market entrants, and options for policy. Fiscal Studies. 2020; 41(3): 549-590.

[17] Konings M. Money as icon. Theory & Event. 2011; 14(3).

[18] Kellermann P. The money paradigm: A sociological view on a

reified symbol. Innovation: The European Journal of Social Science Research. 1994; 7(4): 453-459.

[19] Stiglitz J. The role of the financial system in development. In Presentation at the fourth annual bank conference on development in Latin America and the Caribbean. 1998; 29: 17.

[20] Merton R.C. The financial system and economic performance. In International Competitiveness in Financial Services. 1990: 5-42.

[21] Krueger A. Crisis prevention and resolution: lessons from Argentina. In Speech prepared for National Bureau of Economic Research Conference on the Argentina Crisis. July 2002; 17. Cambridge, Mass.

[22] Spruk R. The rise and fall of Argentina. Latin American Economic Review.2019; 28(1): 1-40.

[23] Argentina Foreign Exchange Reserves. TradingEconomics. https://tradingeconomics.com/argentina/foreign-exchange-reserves.

[24] Argentines have US$250 billion stashed outside financial system, says INDEC. Beunos Aires Times. 2021.

[25] Van Raaij W.F., Gianotten H.J. Consumer confidence, expenditure, saving, and credit. Journal of Economic Psychology.1990; 11(2): 269-290.

[26] Gershenfeld J.E.C., Brooks D., Mulloy M. The decline and resurgence of the US auto industry. Journal-Economic Policy Institute. 2015.

[27] Baily M.N., Farrell D., Greenberg E., et al. Increasing global competition and labor productivity: Lessons from the US automotive industry. McKensie Global Institute. 2005.

[28] Huillén M.F. The global economic & financial crisis: A timeline. The Lauder Institute, University of Pennsylvania. 2009: 1-91.

[29] Goolsbee A.D., Krueger A.B. A retrospective look at rescuing

and restructuring General Motors and Chrysler. Journal of Economic Perspectives. 2015; 29(2): 3-24.

[30] Quelch J.A., Jocz K.E. How to market in a downturn. Harvard Business Review. 2009; 87(4): 52-62.

[31] Steenkamp J.B.E., Fang E. The impact of economic contractions on the effectiveness of R&D and advertising: Evidence from US companies spanning three decades. Marketing Science. 2011; 30(4): 628-645.

[32] Caballero R.J., Hammour M.L. On the Timing and Efficiency of Creative Destruction. The Quarterly Journal of Economics. 1996; 111(3): 805–852.

[33] Tonkiss F. Trust, confidence and economic crisis. Intereconomics.2009; 44(4): 196-202.

Chapter 4

[1] Asimov I. Three laws of robotics. Runaround; 1941.

[2] McCauley L. The Frankenstein complex and Asimov's three laws. In Association for the Advancement of Artificial Intelligence. November 2007. https://www.aaai.org/Papers/Workshops/2007/WS-07-07/WS07-07-003.pdf.

[3] Palumbo D. Alex Proyas's I, robot: Much more faithful to Asimov than you think. Journal of the Fantastic in the Arts. 2011; 22(1).

[4] Berger E., Israel G., Miller C., Parkinson B., Reeves A., Williams N. World History: Cultures, States, and Societies to 1500; 2016.

[5] Algaze, G. The end of prehistory and the Uruk period. The Sumerian World. Routledge; 2013: 92-118.

[6] Fonte G. Energy Management Reduces Great Pyramid Build Effort by More Than 98%. Journal of Construction Engineering and Management. 2011; 137(12): 1195-1204.

[7] Number of Ford employees from FY 2018, by region. Statista. https://www.statista.com/statistics/741379/number-of-ford-employees-by-region/.

[8] Ford Motor Company's vehicle sales at wholesale from FY 2009 to FY 2021. Statista.
https://www.statista.com/statistics/297315/ford-vehicle-sales/.

[9] Isaacson W. Steve Jobs, Simon & Schuster; 2011.

[10] Wozniak S. Iwoz: Computer geek to cult icon. WW Norton & Company; 2007.

[11] Luke Dormehl today in Apple history: Steve Jobs visits the Soviet Union. July 4, 2022.
https://www.cultofmac.com/436469/today-in-apple-history-steve-jobs-visits-the-soviet-union/#:~:text=Isaacson%20wrote%20that%20Jobs%20%E2%80%9Cinsist ed,KGB%20agent%20allegedly%20told%20Jobs.

[12] Thatcher I.D. Trotsky. Routledge; 2005.

[13] Gallo R. Who killed Leon Trotsky? Princeton University Library Chronicle. 2013; 75(1): 109-118.

[14] Aworawo D. The road not taken: Political action and the crisis of democratic values and stability in post-independence Equatorial Guinea. Critical Issues in Justice and Politics.2012: 71.

[15] Cronjé S. Equatorial Guinea, the Forgotten Dictatorship: Forced Labour and Political Murder in Central Africa. United Kingdom, Anti-Slavery Society, 1976.

[16] Murray D. The Top 16 Richest World Leaders and Their Net Worth. April 3, 2018. https://www.slice.ca/the-top-16-richest-world-leaders-and-their-net-worth/.

[18]Shaxson N. What caring neighbors do? The Virginia Quarterly Review. 2007; 83(1):34-XIV.
https://www.proquest.com/scholarly-journals/what-caring-neighbors-do/docview/205378307/se-2.

[19] McSherry B. The political economy of oil in Equatorial Guinea. African Studies Quarterly.2006; 8(3).

[20] Equatorial Guinea: Palace in the jungle: Ordinary folk see none of their country's riches. The Economist March 12, 2016. https://www.economist.com/middle-east-and-africa/2016/03/10/palace-in-the-jungle

[21] Nsehe M. An African Dictator's Son and His Very Lavish Toys. Forbes. July 7, 2011. https://www.forbes.com/sites/mfonobongnsehe/2011/07/07/an-african-dictators-son-and-his-very-lavish-toys/?sh=5f9be2d5598d

[22] Sellmeyer D. 11 Supercars of Teodoro Obiang Nguema Mbasogo Seized by French Police. September 29, 2011. https://gtspirit.com/2011/09/29/11-supercars-of-teodoro-obiang-nguema-mbasogo-seized-by-french-police/.

[23] Equatorial Guinea's web of wealth and repression. https://issafrica.org/about-us/press-releases/equatorial-guineas-web-of-wealth-and-repression.

[24] Equatorial Guinea – Human Development Report 2020. United Nations Development Programme. 2020. https://hdr.undp.org/sites/default/files/Country-Profiles/GNQ.pdf

[25] Equatorial Guinea – Human Development Report 2022. BTI Transformation Index. https://bti-project.org/fileadmin/api/content/en/downloads/reports/country_report_2022_GNQ.pdf

[26] Gardner, D. The Pariah President: Teodoro Obiang is a brutal dictator responsible for thousands of deaths. So why is he treated like an elder statesman on the world stage? Archived from the original on 12 June 2008. The Ottawa Citizen (reprint: dangardner.ca). 2005.

[27] Vines A. Well oiled: oil and human rights in Equatorial Guinea. Human Rights Watch; 2009.

[28] Aprokomania. Ten Facts You Probably Didn't Know About Africa's Longest Serving Dictator by aprokomania(m). https://www.nairaland.com/1932323/ten-facts-probably-didnt-know. Published October 3, 2014.

[29] Equatorial Guinea Background Info. Archived from the original on March 9, 2007. Lonely Planet. 2007.

[30] Roberts A. The Wonga Coup. Public Affairs; 2006.

[31] Kenyon P. Dictatorland: The men who stole Africa. London: Head of Zeus; 2018.

[32] Artucio A. The trial of Macias in Equatorial Guinea. International Commission of Jurists. 1979: 6–8.

[33] North Korea – A country study. Library of Congress Country Studies. 2009.

[34] Yeo A. State, Society and Markets in North Korea. Cambridge University Press; 2021.

[35] Xiang Q. The black markets of North Korea. Modern Economy. 2019; 10(07): 1759.

[36] Choe S.T. The new markets of North Korea: Jangmadang. American Journal of Management. 2015; 15(4): 62.

[37] Zhang W., Lee M. Black markets, red states: Media piracy in China and the Korean Wave in North Korea. In South Korean popular culture and North Korea. Routledge; 2019: 83-95.

[38] Sang-Hun C. North Korea Revalues Its Currency. Archived from the original on May 21, 2013. North Korea. The New York Times. 2009.

[39] Widespread anger as N. Korea limits currency exchange. Chosun Ilbo. December 7, 2009. https://reliefweb.int/report/democratic-peoples-republic-korea/widespread-anger-nkorea-limits-currency-exchange#:~:text=North%20Koreans%20are%20allowed%20to,sources%20in% 20the%20communist%20country

[40] Harden B. North Korea revalues currency, destroying personal savings. The Washington Post. December 2, 2009.

[41] Oh K. Korea's path from poverty to philanthropy. The Korea Times. 2010.

[42] Heo U., Jeon H., Kim H., Kim O. The political economy of South Korea: economic growth, democratization, and financial crisis. Maryland Series in Contemporary Asian Studies. 2008; (2): 1.

[43] Gills B. North Korea and the crisis of socialism: the historical ironies of national division. Third World Quarterly.1992; 13(1): 107-130.

[44] Chaudhuri S. Government and economic development in South Korea, 1961-79. Social Scientist.1996: 18-35.

[45] Kim H.A. Korea's Development under Park Chung Hee. Routledge; 2004. https://www.taylorfrancis.com/books/mono/10.4324/9780203356425/korea-development-park-chung-hee-hyung-kim.

[46] The Korean Economy. Korean Cultural Center. https://www.koreanculture.org/korea-information-economy.

[47] The World Bank. GDP (current US$) - Korea, Rep. World. https://data.worldbank.org/indicator/NY.GDP.MKTP.CD?locations=KR

[48] The Heritage Foundation. South Korea. https://www.heritage.org/index/country/southkorea/

[49] North Korea. The World Factbook. Central Intelligence Agency. 2022. https://www.cia.gov/the-world-factbook/countries/korea-north/

[50] Knight R. Are North Koreans really three inches shorter than South Koreans. BBC News, 2012. https://www.bbc.com/news/magazine-17774210

[51] 임정요. South Koreans live 11 years longer than North Koreans: report. November 3, 2016.
http://www.koreaherald.com/view.php?ud=20161103000182.

[52] Weber M. Politik als beruf. Vol. 2. Duncker & Humblot, 1926.

[53] Ingiriis M.H. Suicidal state in Somalia: The rise and fall of the Siad Barre regime, 1969–1991. UPA; 2016.

[54] Terdiman M. Somalia at war: between radical Islam and tribal politics. S. Daniel Abraham Center for International and Regional Studies, Tel Aviv University. 2008.

[55] Sucin S. Somalia operations: Lessons to be learned by the United Nations and United States. Zb. Radova.1995; 32: 171.

[56] In Somalia, UN official urges massive response for world's 'worst humanitarian disaster', UN News. July 11, 2011.

[57] Hironaka A. Neverending Wars: The International Community, Weak States, and the Perpetuation of Civil War. Harvard University Press: Cambridge, Mass; 2005: 3.

Chapter 5

[1] Wallace D. The Jedi Path: A Manual for Students of the Force. Becker & Mayer; 2012.

[2] Lucasfilm Ltd. Star Wars vol 1-6. 20th Century Fox: Beverly Hills, California, US. 1977-2005.

[3] Huberman M., Minns, C. The times they are not changin': Days and hours of work in Old and New Worlds, 1870–2000. Explorations in Economic History. 2007; 44: 538-567.

[4] Rignall J. One Hot Summer: Dickens, Darwin, Disraeli, and the Great Stink of 1858. The George Eliot Review. 2018; 49: 107-6.

[5] Corton C.L. London fog: the biography. Harvard University Press; 2015.

[6] Mandel E. Formation of Econ Thought of Karl Marx. NYU

Press; 1971.

[7] Veblen T. The socialist economics of Karl Marx and his followers. The Quarterly Journal of Economics.1907; 21(2): 299-322.

[8] Rosenberg N. Karl Marx on the economic role of science. Journal of Political Economy. 1974; 82(4): 713-728.

[9] Aluf I.A. February Bourgeois Democratic Revolution of 1917: The Great Soviet Encyclopedia. 3rd ed. The Gale Group, Inc; 1979.

[10] Carr E.H., Davies R.W. The Russian Revolution: From Lenin to Stalin (1917-1929). London: Macmillan; 1979.

[11] Tauger M.B. Stalin, Soviet Agriculture, and Collectivisation. Food and conflict in Europe in the age of the two World Wars. (pp. 109-142) Palgrave Macmillan, London; 2006

[12] Kotkin S. Stalin: Paradoxes of Power, 1878–1928. London: Allen Lane; 2014.

[13] Johnson I.O. Blood-Soaked Monster - Stalin Vol. 1 by Stephen Kotkin. Claremont Review of Books. 2018; 18 (4).

[14] Schmemann S. From Czarist Rubble, a Russian Autocrat Rises. Review of Stalin: Paradoxes of Power' by Stephen Kotkin. The New York Times. 2015.

[15] Pipes R. The Cleverness of Joseph Stalin. NYT Review of Books; 2014.

[16] Gessen K. How Stalin Became Stalinist. The New Yorker. 2017.

[17] Stalin J. Report to the 17th party congress on the work of the central committee of the all-Union Communist Party (Bolsheviks), January 26, 1934. In: Stalin J. Writings Volume 13. Moscow: State Publishing House of Political Literature; 1951: 282.

[18] Jasny N. Soviet industrialization, 1928–1952. Chicago, IL: University of Chicago Press; 1961.

[19] Grossman G. Thirty years of Soviet industrialization. Soviet Survey 26. 1958: 15–21.

[20] Ofer G. Soviet economic growth: 1928-1985. Journal of economic literature.1987; 25(4): 1767-1833.

[21] Bruisch K., Gestwa K. Expertise and the quest for rural modernization in the Russian empire and the Soviet Union. Cahiers du monde russe. Russie-Empire russe-Union soviétique et États indépendants. 2016; 57(57/1): 7-30.

[22] Dando W.A., & Schlichting J.D. Soviet agriculture today: insights, analyses, and commentary. 1987.

[23] Anderson B.A., Silver B.D. Infant mortality in the Soviet Union: regional differences and measurement issues. Population and Development Review.1986: 705-738.

[24] O'Neill A. Life expectancy in Russia, 1845-2020. 2022. https://www.statista.com/statistics/1041395/life-expectancy-russia-all-time/#:~:text=Between%201945%20and%201950%2C%20Russian,again%20in%20more%20recent%20years.

[25] Klehr H. The Heyday of American Communism: The Depression Decade. Basic Books; 1984: 3–5

[26] Avakumovic I. The Communist Party in Canada: A History. Toronto: McClelland and Stewart; 1975.

[27] Dixon K. The Growth of a 'Popular' Japanese Communist Party. Pacific Affairs. 1974; 45(3): 387–402.

[28] Briggs A. The history of broadcasting in the United Kingdom: Volume I: The birth of broadcasting (Vol. 1). Oxford University Press; 1995.

[29] Burns T. The BBC: Public Institution and Private World. Springer; 2016.

[30] Lyth P. The Empire's airway: British civil aviation from 1919 to

1939. Revue belge de philologie et d'histoire. 2000; 78(3): 865-887.

[31] Lyth P. Chosen Instruments: The Evolution of British Airways. In Flying the Flag. Palgrave Macmillan, London; 1998: 50-86.

[32] Why nationalisation has fallen out of favour in Britain. The performance of state-owned industries has fallen over time. December 2, 2015. https://www.economist.com/the-economist-explains/2015/12/02/why-nationalisation-has-fallen-out-of-favour-in-britain.

[33] Schmidt V. Running on empty: the end of dirigisme in French economic leadership. Modern & Contemporary France. 1997; 5(2): 229-41.

[34] Li C.P. Rising East Asia: The Quest for Governance, Prosperity, and Security. CQ Press; 2020.

[35] Eichengreen B., Uzan M. The Marshall Plan: economic effects and implications for Eastern Europe and the former USSR. Economic Policy. 1992; 7(14): 13-75.

[36] Kunz D.B. The Marshall Plan reconsidered: a complex of motives. Foreign Affairs.1997; 76(3): 162-170.

[37] Livi-Bacci M. On the human costs of collectivization in the Soviet Union. Population and Development Review.1993: 743-766.

[38] Markevich A., Naumenko N., Qian N. The political-economic causes of the Soviet great famine, 1932–33. National Bureau of Economic Research. 2021; 29089.

[39] Ravallion M. Famines and economics. Journal of Economic Literature. 1997; 35(3): 1205-1242.

[40] Grant T. Russia: From Revolution to Counter-revolution. Wellred Books; 1997.

[41] Rossman J.J., Rossman J.J. Worker resistance under Stalin: class and revolution on the shop floor (Vol. 96). Harvard University Press; 2009.

[42] Filtzer D. Soviet Workers and de-Stalinization. Cambridge: Cambridge University Press; 1992.

[43] Grossman G. The second economy in the USSR. Problems of Communism. 1997; 26(5): 25-40.

[44] Treml V.G., Alexeev M.V. The second economy and the destabilization effect of its growth on the state economy in the Soviet Union: 1965-1989. Berkeley-Duke Occasional Papers.1993.

[45] Ivanova G.M., Raleigh D.J., Mikhailovna G., Flath C.A. Labor Camp Socialism: The Gulag in the Soviet Totalitarian System: The Gulag in the Soviet Totalitarian System. Routledge; 2015.

[46] Conquest R. Victims of Stalinism: a comment. Europe-Asia Studies. 1997; 49(7): 1317-9.

[47] Reiman M. About Russia, Its Revolutions, Its Development and Its Present. Peter Lang International Academic Publishers; 2016.

[48] Phillips P.J.J. Gagging on profundity. Victoria: Friesen Press; 2013.

[49] Jokes about rulers. http://www.allrussias.com/jokes/section_jokes_02.asp.

[50] Healey D. Golfo Alexopoulos. Illness and Inhumanity in Stalin's Gulag. 2018: 1049-1051.

[51] Getty J.A., Getty J.A. Origins of the great purges: the Soviet Communist Party reconsidered, 1933-1938 (No. 43). Cambridge University Press; 1987.

[52] Shatz M. (1984). Stalin, the great purge, and Russian history: a new look at the "new class". The Carl Beck Papers in Russian and East European Studies. 1984; (305): 48.

[53] Maddison A. Statistics on World Population, GDP and Per Capita GDP, 1-2008 AD. https://web.archive.org/web/20211102093357/http%3A%2F%2Fwww.ggdc.net%2Fmaddison%2Foriindex.htm

[54] Brainerd E. Reassessing the standard of living in the Soviet Union: an analysis using archival and anthropometric data. The Journal of Economic History.2010; 70(1): 83-117.

[55] Ofer G. Soviet Economic Growth: 1928-1985. RAND/UCLA. Center for the Study of Soviet International Behavior.1988; 5.

[56] Angus M. Development Centre Studies the World Economy a Millennial Perspective: A Millennial Perspective. OECD Publishing; 2001.

[57] Vidyarthi K. Glasnost and Perestroika: Did Gorbachev Break the USSR? Britannica; 2016. Available at SSRN 2755245.

[58] Miller C. The struggle to save the Soviet economy: Mikhail Gorbachev and the collapse of the USSR. UNC Press Books; 2016.

[59] Nove A. Economic History of the USSR. London: Allen Lane; 1969.

[60] Doniger W. On Hinduism. Oxford University Press; 2014.

[61] Smith D. Hinduism. In Religions in the Modern World. Routledge; 2016: 57-88.

[62] Wilson R. Economics, Ethics and Religion: Jewish, Christian and Muslim Economic Thought. Durham, NC: Macmillan; 1997.

[63] Krawchuk A. Orthodox Christianity and Islam on economic justice: Universal ideals and contextual challenges in Russia. In Poverty and Wealth in Judaism, Christianity, and Islam. Palgrave Macmillan, New York; 2016: 127-152.

[64] Sachs J. The Price of Civilization. New York: Random House; 2011: 112.

[65] Fang L. Where Have All the Lobbyists Gone? The Nation. February 19, 2014

[66] Bukhari J. Wall Street Spent $2 Billion Trying to Influence the 2016 Election. Fortune. March 8, 2017.

[67] Harris P. America is better than this': paralysis at the top leaves voters desperate for change". The Guardian. 2011.

[68] Martin A. Inside the powerful lobby fighting for your right to eat pizza. Bloomberg.2015.

[69] Dell Antonia K.J. Lobbying against the too-healthy school lunch. Slate Magazine. 2011

[70] Mulligan C.B. Financial Lobbying and the Housing Crisis. The study by the I.M.F. economists found that the heaviest lobbying came from lenders making riskier loans. The New York Times. 2011.

[71] Collins T.M., Gitelman L., Jankunis G. Thomas Edison and Modern America. Boston: Palgrave Macmillan; 2002.

[72] Benca J. Tests shine light on the secret of the Livermore light bulb. The Mercury News. February 3, 2011.

[73] Krajewski M. The Great Lightbulb Conspiracy. IEEE Spectrum. 2014.

[74] Friedel R. Obsolescence: origins and outrages. Technology and Culture. 2013; 54(1): 167-9.

[75] Jovinelly J., Netelkos J. The Crafts and Culture of a Medieval Guild. Rosen; 2006: 8.

[76] Davidson T. A History of Education. Charles Scribner's Sons, New York; 1900.

[77] Yee T., Boukus E., Cross D., Samuel D. Primary care workforce shortages: Nurse practitioner scope-of-practice laws and payment policies. National Institute for Health Care Reform Research Brief. 2013 Feb 1; 13: 1-7.

[78] Reed T. Turf wars heat up after pandemic blurred provider treatment lines. Axios Vitals. April 13, 2022. https://www.axios.com/2022/04/13/turf-wars-heat-up-between-doctors-and-nurse-practitioners

[79] Murray D., Prynn J.P., eds. TfL Tube strike: Total shutdown of Tube set to cost London £300 million. July 9, 2015. https://www.standard.co.uk/news/transport/tfl-tube-strike-total-shutdown-of-tube-set-to-cost-london-ps300-million-10377756.html.

[80] National Library of Australia. The Costigan report. The Canberra Times.1984; 59(17): 932.

[81] Charbonneau commission finds corruption widespread in Quebec's construction sector. November 25, 2015. https://www.cbc.ca/news/canada/montreal/charbonneau-corruption-inquiry-findings-released-1.3331577.

[82] Jamison S.W., Brereton J.P. eds. The Rigveda: the earliest religious poetry of India. South Asia Research; 2014.

[83] Tower Hamlets' Local History Library and Archives. White slavery in London. The Link; 21.

[84] Raw L. Striking a Light: The Bryant and May Matchwomen and their Place in History. London: Continuum International; 2011.

[85] Kowal T. The role of the prison guards union in California's troubled prison system. California Policy Centre. June 15, 2011

[86] CCPOA.org - California Correctional Peace Officers Association (official website)

[87] Petersilia J. Understanding California corrections. California Policy Research Center.2006; 15(1).

[88] Green N. From Rome to Rome: The Evolution of Competition Law into a Twenty-First Century Religion. Competititon LJ. 2010; 9: 7.

[89] Darcy v Allin (1602) Noy 173, KB, 182.

[90] Federal Trade Commission. The Antitrust Laws.

[91] Independence Hall Association: US History. The New Tycoons: John D. Rockefeller. The Gilded Age.

https://www.ushistory.org/us/36b.asp.

[92] U.S. House of Representatives. The Clayton Antitrust Act. History, Art, and Archives.

[93] Woods W., Wheatley A.C. The Wagner Act Decision – A Charter of Liberty for Labor? Geo. Wash. L. Rev; 1936–1937: 5: 846.

[94] National Labor Relations Act as amended (PDF/details) in the GPO Statute Compilations collection. https://www.govinfo.gov/content/pkg/COMPS-8189/uslm/COMPS-8189.xml.

[95] Wagner S. How Did the Taft-Hartley Act Come About? History News Network.

[96] Jeffries N. The Metropolis Local Management Act and the archaeology of sanitary reform in the London Borough of Lambeth 1856–86. Post-Medieval Archaeology. 2006; 40(2): 272-290.

[97] Saint A. Politics and the people of London: the London County Council (1889–1965). Bloomsbury Academic; 1989.

Chapter 6

[1] Schoenfeld C.G. God the Father—and Mother: Study and Extension of Freud's Conception of God as an Exalted Father. American imago. 1962; 19(3): 213-34.

[2] Berger E., Israel G., Miller C., Parkinson B., Reeves A., Williams N. World History: Cultures, States, and Societies to 1500; 2016.

[3] Kerr M. Kim Jong Un Could Drive at Age 3: North Korea's Most Insane Claims About Its Leaders. June 17, 2018. https://www.cheatsheet.com/culture/kim-jong-il-made-11-holes-in-one-north-koreas-most-insane-claims-about-its-leaders.html/.

[4] Fenton S. Kim Jong-un claims to have cured Aids, Ebola and cancer with single miracle drug. 19 June 2015. https://www.independent.co.uk/news/world/asia/kim-jongun-claims-to-have-cured-aids-ebola-and-cancer-with-single-miracle-

drug-10332386.html.

[5] Nove A. Economic History of the USSR. London: Allen Lane; 1969.

[6] Rand A. What is capitalism? (pp. 11-34). Second Renaissance Book Service; 1967.

[7] Mayhew R. Ayn Rand's Marginalia: Her Critical Comments on the Writings of over 20 Authors. Second Renaissance Pr; 1998

[8] Clark D.G. CS Lewis: A guide to his theology. John Wiley & Sons; 2008.

[9] Genovese E.D. Critical Legal Studies as radical politics and world view. Yale JL & Human. 1991: 131.

[10] Ober J. The original meaning of 'democracy': capacity to do things, not majority rule. Princeton/Stanford Working Papers in Classics Paper, (090704). 2007.

[11] Drew K.F. Magna Carta. Greenwood Publishing Group; 2004.

[12] Breay C., Harrison J., eds. Magna Carta: Law, Liberty, Legacy. London: The British Library; 2015.

[13] Pincus S.C., Robinson J.A. What really happened during the Glorious Revolution? (No. w17206). National Bureau of Economic Research. 2011.

[14] Billias, G.A. American constitutionalism heard round the world, 1776-1989: a global perspective. NYU Press; 2009.

[15] Israel J.I. The Enlightenment that Failed: Ideas, Revolution, and Democratic Defeat, 1748-1830. Oxford University Press. 2019.

[16] Crook M. Elections in the French Revolution: An Apprenticeship in Democracy, 1789-1799. Cambridge University Press; 1996.

[17] Amar A.R. The Fifteenth Amendment and Political Rights. Cardozo L. Rev. 1995; 17: 2225.

[18] Alabama Literacy Test, circa mid-1960s. https://www.crmvet.org/info/litques.pdf

[19] Lee D.R. Voting with Ballots versus Voting with Your Feet. econlib.org. February 5, 2018.

[20] Rome S.H. How we got here: a brief history of voting rights. In Promote the Vote Springer, Cham. 2022; (pp. 51-71).

[21] "History of Federal Voting Rights Laws: The Voting Rights Act of 1965". United States Department of Justice. July 28, 2017. Archived from the original on January 6, 2021.

[22] Dallek R. "Presidency: How Do Historians Evaluate the Administration of Lyndon Johnson?". History News Network. Archived from the original on January 9, 2021.

[23] Tokaji D.P. "The New Vote Denial: Where Election Reform Meets the Voting Rights Act". South Carolina Law Review. 2006; 57.

[24] "Nixon Calls War on Drugs". The Palm Beach Post. June 18, 1971.

[25] Dufton E. "The War on Drugs: How President Nixon Tied Addiction to Crime". The Atlantic. March 26, 2012. Archived from the original on November 5, 2012.

[26] Travis J., Western B., Redburn F.S. The growth of incarceration in the United States: Exploring causes and consequences. 2014.

[27] Uggen C., Larson R., Shannon S. 6 million lost voters: State-level estimates of felony disenfranchisement. Washington, DC: The Sentencing Project. 2016

[28] Curtin J. New Zealand: A country of firsts in women's political rights. In The Palgrave handbook of women's political rights. Palgrave Macmillan, London. 2019; (pp. 129-142).

[29] Marilley S.M. Woman suffrage and the origins of liberal feminism in the United States, 1820-1920. In Woman Suffrage and the

Origins of Liberal Feminism in the United States, 1820-1920. Harvard University Press; 2013.

[30] Mossuz-Lavau J. Women and politics in France. French politics and society, 1992; 1-8.

[31] Bendix J. Women's suffrage and political culture: A modern Swiss case. Women & Politics, 1992; 12(3), 27-56.

[32] Alotaibi F., Cutting R., Morgan J. A critical analysis of the literature in women's leadership in Saudi Arabia. International Journal of Business Administration and Management Research, 2017; 3(1).

[33] Percentage distribution of population in the United States in 2016 and 2060, by race and Hispanic origin. https://www.statista.com/statistics/270272/percentage-of-us-population-by-ethnicities/

[34] Women in the U.S. Senate 2016. https://cawp.rutgers.edu/facts/levels-office/congress/women-us-senate-2016

[35] Vandewalker I. Election spending 2014: Outside spending in senate races since Citizens United. Brennan Center for Justice at New York University School of Law. 2015.

[36] Plato, Sterling R.W., Scott W.C. "Book VII." The Republic. New York: Norton. 1996; 35-261.

[37] Darcy R. Women, elections, and representation. U of Nebraska Press; 1994.

[38] Loewenstein K. Dictatorship and the German constitution: 1933-1937. The University of Chicago Law Review, 1937; 4(4), 537-574.

[39] Lepsius M.R. From fragmented party democracy to government by emergency decree and national socialist takeover: Germany. In Max Weber and Institutional Theory. Springer, Cham. 2017; 111-151.

[40] Thompson M.R. Asia's hybrid dynasties. Asian Affairs. 2012; 43(2), 204-220.

[41] International Churchill Society. "The worst form of government." https://winstonchurchill.org/resources/quotes/the-worst-form-of-government/

[42] Star Trek: The Original Series, "Let That Be Your Last Battlefield." https://www.allgreatquotes.com/star-trek-89/

[43] Knobloch-Westerwick S., Mothes C., Polavin N. Confirmation bias, ingroup bias, and negativity bias in selective exposure to political information. Communication Research. 2020 Feb; 47(1): 104-24.

[44] Millner A., Ollivier H., Simon L. Confirmation bias and signaling in Downsian elections. Journal of Public Economics. 2020 May 1; 185: 104175.

[45] Rose R. Comparing public policy: an overview. European journal of political research. 1973 Apr;1(1):67-94.

[46] Lin J.Y. Policy Responses to the Global Economic Crisis. World Bank. World Bank. 2009.. https://openknowledge.worldbank.org/handle/10986/4602

[47] Claessens M.S., Kose M.A., Laeven M.L., Valencia M.F. Financial crises: Causes, consequences, and policy responses. International Monetary Fund; February 19, 2014.

[48] Béland D., Cantillon B., Hick R., Moreira A. Social policy in the face of a global pandemic: Policy responses to the COVID-19 crisis. Social Policy & Administration. 2021 Mar; 55(2): 249-60.

[49] Hick R., Murphy M.P. Common shock, different paths? Comparing social policy responses to COVID-19 in the UK and Ireland. Social Policy & Administration. 2021 Mar; 55(2): 312-25.

Chapter 7

[1] Wachowski, Lana, and Lilly Wachowski. 1999. The Matrix. United States: Warner Bros.

[2] McLeay M., Amar R., and Ryland T. Money in the modern economy: an introduction. Bank of England. Quarterly Bulletin, vol. 54, no. 1, 2014, pp. 4-13.

[3] Ludwig V.M. The theory of money and credit. New Haven: Yale University Press, 1953. https://mises.org/library/theory-money-and-credit/html

[4] Brunner K., Meltzer A.H. The uses of money: money in the theory of an exchange economy. The American Economic Review. 1971; 61(5): 784-805.

[5] Vierra M.R. Currency and politics: The assignat and its economic correlation with political decisions during the French Revolution, 1789–1796. California State University, Dominguez Hills; 2003.

[6] Bourne H.E. Maximum Prices in France in 1793 and 1794. The American Historical Review. 1917; 23(1), 107-113.

[7] Bignon V., Flandreau M. The Other Way: A Narrative History of the Bank of France. In: Edvinsson R, Jacobson T, Waldenström D, editors. Sveriges Riksbank and the History of Central Banking. Cambridge: Cambridge University Press; 2018. page 206–41.

[8] Gup B.E. What is money? From commodities to virtual currencies/Bitcoin. In The Most Important Concepts in Finance. Edward Elgar Publishing, 2017.

[9] Goldberg D. The Massachusetts paper money of 1690. The Journal of Economic History. 2009; 69(4): 1092-106.

[10] Gu C., Mattesini F., Wright R. Money and credit redux. Econometrica. 2016; 84(1), 1-32.

[11] Selgin G. Synthetic commodity money. Journal of Financial Stability. 2015; 17, 92-99.

[12] Fungáčová Z., Hasan I., Weill L. Trust in banks. Journal of Economic Behavior & Organization. 2019; 157: 452-76.

[13] Carpenter S., Demiralp S. Money, reserves, and the transmission of monetary policy: Does the money multiplier exist? Journal of macroeconomics. 2012; 34(1): 59-75.

[14] Black D.C., Dowd M.R. The money multiplier, the money market, and the LM curve. Eastern Economic Journal. 1994; 20(3): 301-10.

[15] Moore B.J. The endogenous money supply. Journal of Post Keynesian Economics. 1988; 10(3): 372-85.

[16] Gray M.S. Central bank balances and reserve requirements. International Monetary Fund. 2011.

[17] McKenzie G. Loan-loss provisions and bank buffer-stock capital. Applied Financial Economics. 1996; 6(3), 213-223.

[18] Odell K.A., Weidenmier M.D. Real shock, monetary aftershock: The 1906 San Francisco earthquake and the panic of 1907. The Journal of Economic History. 2004; 64(4), 1002-1027.

[19] Sprague O.M. The American crisis of 1907. The Economic Journal. 1908; 18(71): 353-72.

[20] Frydman C., Hilt E., Zhou L.Y. The Panic of 1907: JP Morgan, Trust Companies, and the Impact of the Financial Crisis. Working paper, 2012.http://econ.as.nyu.edu/docs/IO/23161/Hilt_03232012. pdf.

[21] Bruner R.F. The dynamics of a financial dislocation: The panic of 1907 and the Subprime Crisis. Insights into the Global Financial Crisis. 2009; 20: 20.

[22] Bruner R.F., Carr S.D. The panic of 1907: Lessons learned from the market's perfect storm. John Wiley & Sons; 2009.

[23] The Fed's Formative Years: 1913 – 1929. Federal Reserve History. 2013. https://www.federalreservehistory.org/essays/feds-

formative-years

[24] Caton J. Crisis and Credit Allocation: The Effect of Ideology on Monetary Policy during the Great Depression and the Great Recession. AIER Sound Money Project Working Paper. 2020; (2021-02).

[25] Calomiris C.W. Mason J.R. Contagion and Bank Failures During the Great Depression: The June 1932 Chicago Banking Panic. National Bureau of Economic Research Working Paper Series. 1994; 4934

[26] Open Market Investment Committee for the Federal Reserve System. Exhibit A: Policy Governing Open Market Purchases by Federal Reserve Banks and the Administration Thereof as Applied by the Open Market Investment Committee, April 13, 1923. 1923. https://fraser.stlouisfed.org/author/open-market-investment-committee-federal-reserve-system

[27] Steelman A. Full Employment and Balanced Growth Act of 1978 (Humphrey-Hawkins). Federal Reserve History. https://www.federalreservehistory.org/essays/humphrey-hawkins-act

[28] Amadeo K. The Great Depression: What Happened, What Caused It, and How It Ended. The Balance. 2022. https://www.thebalancemoney.com/the-great-depression-of-1929-3306033

[29] Amadeo K. Great Depression Timeline: 1929–1941. The Balance. 2022. https://www.thebalancemoney.com/great-depression-timeline-1929-1941-4048064

[30] Kindleberger C.P. The world in depression, 1929-1939. Univ of California Press; 1986.

[31] Wheelock D.C. The Great Depression: An Overview. The Federal Reserve Bank of St. Louis, September. 2007.

[32] Nicholas T., Scherbina A. Real Estate Prices During the Roaring

Twenties and the Great Depression. Real Estate Economics. 2013; 41(2): 278–309.

[33] Bordo M.D., Landon-Lane J. Does expansionary monetary policy cause asset price booms; some historical and empirical evidence. National Bureau of Economic Research; 2013.

[34] Bernanke B.S., Gertler M. Monetary policy and asset price volatility. National Bureau of Economic Research; 2000.

[35] Bernanke B.S. The Federal Reserve and the financial crisis. 2013 Princeton University Press.

[36] Cecchetti S.G. Crisis and responses: the Federal Reserve in the early stages of the financial crisis. Journal of Economic Perspectives. 2009; 23(1): 51-75.

[37] Carpenter, S.B., Demiralp, S., Eisenschmidt J. The Effectiveness of the Non-standard Policy Measures During the Financial Crises: The Experiences of the Federal Reserve and the European Central Bank. ECB Working Paper No. 1562, European Central Bank. 2013.

[38] The Great Recession: December 2007 – June 2009. Federal Reserve History. www.federalreservehistory.org/essays/great-recession-of-200709

[39] The Crisis, the Fallout, the Change: The Great Recession in Retrospect. Federal Reserve Bank of Cleveland. www.clevelandfed.org/newsroom-and-events/multimedia-storytelling/recession-retrospective.aspx

[40] Harris J.M., Dullien S., Torras M., Roach B., Nelson J.A., Goodwin N. Macroeconomics in Context: A European Perspective. United Kingdom: Taylor & Francis, 2017.

[41] Historical Timeline: The 1930s. FDIC. www.fdic.gov/about/history/timeline/1930s.html

[42] Federal Reserve. Statement on Longer-Run Goals and Monetary Policy Strategy: As adopted effective January 24, 2012.

[43] Haldane A.G., editor. Targeting Inflation: A Conference of Central Banks on the Use of Inflation Targets Organized by the Bank of England, 9-10 March 1995. Bank of England; 1995.

[44] Burdekin R.C., Siklos P.L. Fears of deflation and the role of monetary policy: some lessons and an overview. Deflation: current and historical perspectives. 2004: 1-27.

[45] Singh H., Schumann H. Falling prices: does this cause purchases to be delayed or speed up? Evidence from the gasoline market. Dr. Jeff Mankin, Lipscomb University. 2021: 47.

[46] Gürkaynak R.S, Levin A., Swanson E. Does inflation targeting anchor long-run inflation expectations? Evidence from the US, UK, and Sweden. Journal of the European Economic Association. 2010; 8(6): 1208-42.

[47] Gonçalves C.E, Salles J.M. Inflation targeting in emerging economies: What do the data say? Journal of Development Economics. 2008; 85(1-2): 312-8.

[48] European Central Bank. Greece, Long-term interest rate for convergence purposes. https://sdw.ecb.europa.eu/quickview.do?SERIES_KEY=229.IRS.M.GR.L.L40.CI.0000.EUR.N.Z&periodSortOrder=ASC

[49] Germany Long Term Interest Rate. 1993 – 2022. https://www.ceicdata.com/en/indicator/germany/long-term-interest-rate

[50] Cecioni M., Coenen G., Motto R., Le Bihan H., Ajevskis V., Albertazzi U., Pisani M. The ECB's Price Stability Framework: Past Experience, and Current and Future Challenges. 2021. https://papers.ssrn.com/sol3/papers.cfm?abstract_id=3928290

[51] Trading Economics. Greece Private Debt to GDP. https://tradingeconomics.com/greece/private-debt-to-gdp

[52] Trading Economics. Germany Private Debt to GDP. https://tradingeconomics.com/germany/private-debt-to-gdp

[53] Rady D.A.M. Greece debt crisis: Causes, implications and policy options. Academy of Accounting and Financial Studies Journal. 2012; 16, 87.

[54] Monokroussos P., Thomakos D. Can Greece be saved?: current account, fiscal imbalances and competitiveness. GreeSE papers 2012 (59). Hellenic Observatory, London School of Economics and Political Science, London, UK.

[55] Strupczewski J. Greek 2009 deficit revised higher, euro falls. 2010. https://www.reuters.com/article/us-eu-deficits-idUSTRE63L1G420100422

[56] Trading Economics. Greek Government Budget. https://tradingeconomics.com/greece/government-budget

[57] Panagiotidis T., Printzis P. On the macroeconomic determinants of the housing market in Greece: A VECM approach. International Economics and Economic Policy. 2016; 13(3), 387-409.

[58] Trading Economics. Germany Current Account to GDP. https://tradingeconomics.com/germany/current-account-to-gdp

[59] Trading Economics. Greece GDP. https://tradingeconomics.com/greece/gdp

[60] Coleman J. Greek bailout talks: Are stereotypes of lazy Greeks true? BBC News. 2015; 10.

[61] McDonald C. Are Greeks the hardest workers in Europe? BBC News Magazine. 2012.

[62] Trading Economics. Greek Government Bond 10Y. https://tradingeconomics.com/greece/government-bond-yield

[63] Trading Economics. Greece Gross Minimum Monthly Wage. https://tradingeconomics.com/greece/minimum-wages

[64] Theodoropoulou S. Severe pain, very little gain: internal devaluation and rising unemployment in Greece. Unemployment, internal devaluation and labour market deregulation in Europe.

2016; 25.

[65] Trading Economics. Greece Youth Unemployment Rate. https://tradingeconomics.com/greece/youth-unemployment-rate

[66] Greece GDP 1960-2022. https://www.macrotrends.net/countries/GRC/greece/gdp-gross-domestic-product

Chapter 8

[1] Ball J.A. The zoo hypothesis. Icarus.1973; 19(3); 347-349.

[2] Kane S. More than 100 tribes exist totally isolated from global society. The Independent. 2018. https://www.independent.co.uk/news.

[3] Wade L. From Black Death to fatal flu, past pandemics show why people on the margins suffer most. Science Web site. https://www.science.org/. Published May 14, 2020.

[4] James T. Black Death: The Lasting Impact. BBC Web site. https://www.bbc.co.uk/. February 17, 2011.

[5] The End of Feudalism in J.H.M. Salmon, Society in Crisis: France in the Sixteenth Century. 1979; 19–26

[6] Zentner M.H. The black death and its impact on the church and popular religion. 2015. https://egrove.olemiss.edu/hon_thesis/682/

[7] Ryrie A. The age of Reformation: the Tudor and Stewart realms 1485-1603. Routledge; 2017.

[8] Luther M. The Ninety-Five Theses. Musaicum; 2011.

[9] Eisenstein E.L. The printing press as an agent of change. Cambridge University Press; 1980.

[10] Batchelder R.W., Freudenberger H. On the rational origins of the modern centralized state. Explorations in Economic History. 1983; 20(1): 1.

[11] Nayar S.J. Arms or the man I: gunpowder technology and the early modern romance. Studies in Philology. 2017; 114(3): 517-60.

[12] Wallerstein I. The modern world-system II: Mercantilism and the consolidation of the European world-economy, 1600–1750. Univ of California Press; 2011.

[13] Screpanti E., Zamagni S. The Birth of Political Economy. In Field D.ed. An Outline of the History of Economic Thought. Oxford Academic. 1995; 16-42.

[14] Cook N.D. Born to die: disease and New World conquest, 1492-1650. Cambridge University Press; 1998.

[15] Diamond J.M. Guns, germs and steel: a short history of everybody for the last 13,000 years. Random House; 1998.

[16] LaHaye L. Mercantilism. Library of Economics and Liberty; 2008.

[17] Prak M. ed. Early modern capitalism: economic and social change in Europe 1400-1800 (Vol. 21). Routledge; 2005.

[18] Letiche J.M. Adam Smith and David Ricardo on economic growth. The Punjab University Economist. 1960; 1(2):7-35.

[19] Nachbar T.B. Monopoly, mercantilism, and the politics of regulation. Virginia Law Review. 2005; 91: 1313.

[20] Olsen K. Daily life in 18th-century England. ABC-CLIO; 2017.

[21] Menzies H. The Authentic Adam Smith: His Life and Ideas. Biography. 2007; 30(1): 156-7.

[22] Adam S. The wealth of nations. Aegitas; 2016.

[23] Aitken R., Aitken M. The King Who Lost His Head: The Trial of Charles I. Litig. 2006; 33, 53.

[24] De Krey G.S. Restoration and Revolution in Britain: Political Culture in the Era of Charles II and the Glorious Revolution. Bloomsbury Publishing; 2017.

[25] Ashton TS. The industrial revolution 1760-1830. OUP Catalogue; 1997.

[26] Von Albertini R. The impact of two world wars on the decline of colonialism. Journal of Contemporary History. 1969: 17-35.

[27] Lehning J.R. European colonialism since 1700. Cambridge University Press; 2013.

[28] Štrbáňová S. The Rise of Nazism in Germany and the Second World War. In Holding Hands with Bacteria. Springer, Berlin, Heidelberg. 2016; 61-75

[29] Schain M. The Marshall Plan: Fifty Years After. New York: Palgrave; 2001.

[30] Calomiris C.W. Financial factors in the Great Depression. Journal of Economic Perspectives. 1993; 7(2), 61-85.

[31] Bull H. The great irresponsibles? The United States, the Soviet Union, and world order. International Journal. 1980; 35(3), 437-447.

[32] O'Keefe T.A. Bush II, Obama, and the decline of US hegemony in the Western Hemisphere. Routledge; 2018.

[33] Hirst P. War and power in the twenty-first century: the state, military power and the international system. John Wiley & Sons; 2014.

[34] Kupchan C.A. Isolationism: A History of America's Efforts to Shield Itself from the World. Oxford University Press, USA; 2020.

[35] Kastner S.L., Pearson M.M. Rector C. China and global governance: Opportunistic multilateralism. Global Policy. 2020; 11(1): 164-9.

[36] Mansbach R.W., Ferguson Y.H. The Return of Geopolitics and Declining US Hegemony. In Populism and Globalization 2021 (pp. 89-140). Palgrave Macmillan, Cham.

[37] Barklie G. The impact of the Russia-Ukraine conflict on trade. Special Focus.2022.

[38] Hurd I. International organizations: politics, law, practice. Cambridge University Press; 2020.

[39] Park J., Belderbos R. Patent protection and foreign R&D investment location choices: inventor mobility and policy convergence. Industrial and Corporate Change. 2022; 31(4): 1113-36.

[40] Adach A., Torchio G. Towards a New 'New Deal'? The Past and Future of Transatlantic Cooperation on Privacy Regulation. Amsterdam Review of European Affairs. 2022; 1: 62-75.

[41] Bornstein S.J. Impact of the China-U.S. Trade Deal on Intellectual Property Protection. Greenberg Traurig Web site. January 21, 2020. https://www.gtlaw.com/ en/insights/2020/1/ impact-of-the-china-us-trade-deal-on-intellectual-property-protection.

[42] Martin S. EU to push Australia to clean up petrol standards as part of free trade deal. Guardian News & Media Limited. Sep 1, 2019.

[43] Orbie J., Martens D., Oehri M., Van den Putte L. Promoting sustainable development or legitimising free trade? Civil society mechanisms in EU trade agreements. In Sustainable Development in Africa-EU Relations 2018 (pp. 96-116). Routledge.

[44] OECD. Multinational enterprises in the global economy. May 2018.

[45] Eberlein B. Who fills the global governance gap? Rethinking the roles of business and government in global governance. Organization Studies. 2019 Aug;40(8): 1125-45.

[46] Dass N., Nanda V., Xiao SC. Geographic clustering of corruption in the United States. Journal of Business Ethics. 2021; 173(3): 577-97.

[47] Foreign Corrupt Practices Act. U.S. Department of Justice Web site. www.justice.gov. February 3, 2017.

[48] Yeoh P. The UK Bribery Act 2010: contents and implications. Journal of Financial Crime. 2012.

[49] Spahn E.K. Multijurisdictional Bribery Law Enforcement: The OECD Anti-Bribery Convention. Va. J. Int'l L. 2012; 53, 1.

[50] Botti F., Corsi M., Garraio J., et al. The #metoo social media effect and its potentials for social change in Europe. Brussels: FEPS–Foundation for European Progressive Studies; 2020.

[51] Boulianne S., Lalancette M., Ilkiw D. School strike 4 climate: social media and the international youth protest on climate change. Media and Communication. 2020; 8(2): 208-218.

[52] The Language Conservancy. The loss of our languages. https://languageconservancy.org/language-loss/

[53] Crystal D. Language Death. Cambridge: Cambridge University Press; 2000.

[54] Lyons D. The 10 Most Spoken Languages In The World. Babbel Magazine. 2021.

[55] W3Techs. Usage statistics of content languages for websites. https://w3techs.com/technologies/overview/content_language

[56] Liu Q. A Brief Analysis of the Application of Computer Aided Translation Tools in English Translation. In Journal of Physics: Conference Series 2020 Oct 1. Vol. 1648, No. 3, p. 032005. IOP Publishing.

[57] Desilver D. Despite global concerns about democracy, more than half of countries are democratic. Pew Research Center. 2022. https://www.pewresearch.org/fact-tank/2019/05/14/more-than-half-of-countries-are-democratic/

[58] Milson A. 'Flawed' U.S. Falls Down List of World's Most Democratic Countries. Bloomberg.com. February 10, 2022.

[59] World Bank. Poverty and shared prosperity 2018: Piecing together the poverty puzzle. Washington DC: The World Bank; 2018.

[60] Kharas H. The unprecedented expansion of the global middle class: An update. Brookings Institute. 2017.

[61] Kharas H., Hamel, K. A global tipping point: Half the world is now middle class or wealthier. Brookings Institute. 2018.

[62] Roser M., Ortiz-Ospina E. Literacy. Our World in Data. 2018. https://ourworldindata.org/literacy.

[63] Roser M., Ortiz-Ospina E., Ritchie H. Life expectancy. Our World in Data. October 2019. https://ourworldindata.org/life-expectancy.

[64] Roser M., Ritchie H., Dadonaite B. Child and infant mortality. Our World in Data. November 2019. https://ourworldindata.org/child-mortality.

[65] Peterson D.L., Powers T. Women as drivers of economic growth. Horizons: Journal of International Relations and Sustainable Development. 2019; (14), 176-183.

[66] Women's status and fertility rates. World Population History. 2016. https://worldpopulationhistory.org/womens-status-and-fertility-rates/

[67] OECD, Gender Equality in Education, Employment and Entrepreneurship: Final Report to the MCM 2012. p. 3. http://www.oecd.org/employment/50423364.pdf.

[68] Sánchez-Páramo C., Hill R., Mahler D.G., Narayan A., Yonzan N. COVID-19 leaves a legacy of rising poverty and widening inequality. World Bank.2021. https://worldbank.org/developmenttalk/covid-19-leaves-legacy-rising-poverty-andwidening-inequality.

[69] National Poverty in America Awareness Month: January 2022. The United States Census Bureau.

https://www.census.gov/newsroom/stories/poverty-awareness-month.html

[70] Decerf B. Combining absolute and relative poverty: income poverty measurement with two poverty lines. Social Choice and Welfare. 2021; 56(2): 325-62.

[71] Kuhlmann D. Coveting your neighbour's house: understanding the positional nature of residential satisfaction. Housing Studies. 2020; 35(6): 1142-1162.

[72] Jebb A.T., Tay L., Diener E., Oishi S. Happiness, income satiation and turning points around the world. Nature Human Behaviour. 2018; 2(1): 33-38.

[73] Saadi-Sedik T., Xu R. A vicious cycle: How pandemics lead to economic despair and social unrest. Available at SSRN 3744683. 2020.

[74] Islam M.R., McGillivray M. Wealth inequality, governance and economic growth. Economic Modelling. 2020; 88: 1-3.

[75] Jetin B. Citation: B. Jetin (2016). Reduction of absolute poverty, increase of relative poverty and growing inequalities: a threat to social cohesion in ASEAN countries. In B. Jetin and M. Mikic editors:ASEAN Economic Community 2015: A model for Asia-wide regional integration? Palgrave McMillan, Basingstoke and New York: Palgrave.

[76] Huh H.S., Park C.Y. A new index of globalisation: Measuring impacts of integration on economic growth and income inequality. The World Economy. 2021; 44(2): 409-43.

[77] Cosentino G. Social media and the post-truth world order. London; Cham: Palgrave Pivot; 2020.

[78] Scanni M.S.G. The Great Recession vs The Covid-19 Pandemic: Unemployment and Implications for Public Policy. Thesis. Levy Economics Institute of Bard College; 2021.

[79] Tsegaye K.K. Stay at home: Coronavirus (COVID-19),

isolationism and the future of globalization. African Journal of Political Science and International Relations. 2020; 14(3): 84-90.

[80] Buheji M., Vovk Korže A., Eidan S, Abdulkareem T., Perepelkin N., Mavric B., Preis J., Bartula M., Ahmed D., Buheji A., Chetiayein T. Optimising pandemic response through self-sufficiency-a review paper. American Journal of Economics. 2020;10(5): 277-83.

[81] Bieber F. Global nationalism in times of the COVID-19 pandemic. Nationalities Papers. 2022 Jan; 50(1): 13-25.

[82] Kose M.A., Nagle P.S., Ohnsorge F., Sugawara N. What has been the impact of COVID-19 on debt? Turning a wave into a tsunami. CEPR Discussion Paper No. DP16775. 2022.

[83] United Nations High Commissioner for Refugees. Global Trends Forced Displacement In 2019. https://www.unhcr.org/be/wp-content/uploads/sites/46/2020/07/Global-Trends-Report-2019.pdf.

[84] Ida T. Climate refugees – the world's forgotten victims. World Economic Forum. 2021.

[85] Barrett P., Chen S. The Economics of Social Unrest. International Monetary Fund Web site. August 2021. https://www.imf.org/external/pubs/ft/fandd/2021/08/economics-of-social-unrest-imf-barrett-chen.htm#authors.

[86] Solt F. Diversionary nationalism: Economic inequality and the formation of national pride. The Journal of Politics. 2011; 73(3): 821-30.

[87] Smith A. The theory of moral sentiments. Penguin; 2010.

[88] Nobel economics prize goes to natural experiments pioneers.Inquirer.net. October 11, 2021. https://newsinfo.inquirer.net/1500257/nobel-economics-prize-goes-to-natural-experiments-pioneers.

[89] Skidelsky R. John Maynard Keynes: 1883–1946: Economist,

Philosopher, Statesman. Pan MacMillan; 2003.

[90] Lundberg E. The rise and fall of the Swedish model. Journal of economic literature. 1985; 23(1): 1-36.

[91] Dunne J.P. Military keynesianism: An assessment. In Cooperation for a Peaceful and Sustainable World Part 2. Emerald Group Publishing Limited. 2013; Vol. 20, pp. 117-129.

[92] Evans A.B. Soviet Marxism-Leninism: The Decline of an Ideology. Santa Barbara: ABC-CLIO; 1993.

[93] Busky D.F. Democratic Socialism: A Global Survey. Praeger; 2000: pp. 6–8.

[94] Weintraub S. The Keynesian Light that Failed. Nebraska Journal of Economics and Business. 1975; 14(4): 3-20.

[95] Federal Reserve History. Oil Shock of 1973–74. November 22, 2013. https://www.federalreservehistory.org/essays/oil-shock-of-1973-74.

[96] Jahan S., Mahmud A.S., Papageorgiou C. What Is Keynesian Economics? Finance & Development. 2014; 51 (3). https://www.imf.org/external/pubs/ft/fandd/2014/09/basics.htm

[97] Deeds C. Reaganomics and Thatcherism. Origins, Similarities and Differences. In Atherton, J. (Ed.), GB and US: How far? How close? Presses universitaires François-Rabelais. 1986

[98] Stepney P. The legacy of Margaret Thatcher—A critical assessment. Open Journal of Social Sciences. 2014.

[99] Boskin M.J., Stein H. Reagan and the economy: The successes, failures, and unfinished agenda. ICS Press, Institute for Contemporary Studies; 1987.

[100] Hall M. U.S. Presidents and the Largest Budget Deficits. Investopedia Web site. Updated May 15, 2022. https://www.investopedia.com/

[101] House C.L., Proebsting C., Tesar L.L. Austerity in the Aftermath of the Great Recession. Journal of Monetary Economics. 2020; 115: 37-63.

[102] Furman J. The fiscal response to the Great Recession: Steps taken, paths rejected, and lessons for next time. InFirst responders 2020 (pp. 451-488). Yale University Press.

[103] COVID-19 to Plunge Global Economy into Worst Recession since World War II". World Bank. June 8, 2020. https://www.worldbank.org/en/news/press-release/2020.

[104] Makin A.J., Layton A. The global fiscal response to COVID-19: Risks and repercussions. Economic Analysis and Policy. 2021; 69: 340-9.

[105] Grasselli M.R. Monetary policy responses to covid-19: a comparison with the 2008 crisis and implications for the future of central banking. Review of Political Economy. 2022; 34(3): 420-45.

Chapter 9

[1] Gomes V. The Science Behind "Blade Runner"'s Voight-Kampff Test. Nautilus Web site. https://nautil.us/the-science-behind-blade-runners-voight_kampff-test-2-8353/.July 25, 2019.

[2] Scott, Ridley. 1982. Blade Runner. United States: Warner Bros.

[3] Walker W., van Daalen C. System models for policy analysis. Public Policy Analysis.2013: 157-184. doi 10.1007/978-1-4614-4602-6_7.

[4] Kaufman B.E. Institutional economics and the minimum wage: broadening the theoretical and policy debate. ILR Review. 2010; 63(3): 427-453.

[5] Clemens J., Wither M. The minimum wage and the Great Recession: Evidence of effects on the employment and income trajectories of low-skilled workers. Journal of Public Economics. 2019; 170: 53-67.

[6] Aaronson D. Price pass-through and the minimum wage. Review of Economics and statistics. 2001; 83(1): 158-69.

[7] Lemos S. A Survey of the Effects of the Minimum Wage on Prices. Journal of Economic Surveys. 2008 Feb; 22(1): 187-212.

[8] Kotios A., Pavlidis G., Galanos G. Greece and the Euro: The chronicle of an expected collapse. Intereconomics. 2011; 46(5): 263-269.

[9] International Labour Organization. Monitoring the effects of minimum wages: Effects on Government Finances. International Labour Organization (ILO) Web site. 2022. https://www.ilo.org/.

[10] Zemanek H. Competitiveness within the euro area: the problem that still needs to be solved. Economic Affairs. 2010; 30(3): 42-7.

[11] Kanellopoulos C.N. The effects of minimum wages on wages and employment. Bank of Greece Economic Bulletin. 2015 Jul 1(41).

[12] Trading Economics. Greece Gross Minimum Monthly Wage. https://tradingeconomics.com/greece/minimum-wages

[13] Card D., Krueger A.B. Minimum wages and employment: A case study of the fast food industry in New Jersey and Pennsylvania. National Bureau of Economic Research. 1993.

[14] Wells P. Modigliani on flexible wages and prices. Journal of Post Keynesian Economics.1979; 2(1): 83–93.

[15] Smith J. How compensation and benefits can motivate employees. Canadian HR Reporter. Aug 17, 2021.

[16] Douglas E.J., Shepherd D.A. Self-employment as a career choice: Attitudes, entrepreneurial intentions, and utility maximization. Entrepreneurship theory and practice. 2002; 26(3): 81-90.

[17] Will, S., & Madeleine, S. Immigration and the Labour Market: Theory, Evidence and Policy. Migration Policy Institute;2009.

[18] Anker R. Estimating a living wage: A methodological review.

Geneva: ILO; 2011.

[19] Lacroix R., Dussault F. The spillover effect of public-sector wage contracts in Canada. The Review of Economics and Statistics. 1984: 509-12.

[20] Monastiriotis V. Raising the minimum wage in Greece. Impact case study. London School of Economics and Political Science. 2021.

[21] Wiles R.C. The theory of wages in later English mercantilism. The Economic History Review. 1968; 21(1): 113-126.

[22] Meer J., West J. Effects of the minimum wage on employment dynamics. Journal of Human Resources. 2016; 51(2): 500-22.

[23] Haepp T., Lin C. How does the minimum wage affect firm investments in fixed and human capital? Evidence from China. Review of Development Economics. 2017; 21(4): 1057-80.

[24] Askenazy P. Minimum wage, exports and growth. European Economic Review. 2003; 47(1): 147-64.

ABOUT THE AUTHOR

Dan Hicks lives in Australia not far from Melbourne. He loves movies, his family and his dog. He has qualifications in business, finance and economics and has spent a big part of his adult life trying to understand economics - this is what he thinks he's figured out so far.

He would love to hear what you think of his book. Please leave a review where you bought it.